Brave. Black. First.

50+ African American Women Who Changed the World

Cheryl Willis Hudson

Illustrations by Erin K. Robinson

A Yearling Book

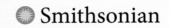

NATIONAL MUSEUM
of AFRICAN AMERICAN
HISTORY & CULTURE

Smithsonian

For all the women who were brave, Black, first—
especially my mom, Lillian Watson Willis

—C.W.H.

For all the magical women in my life . . . the fearless change makers
who guided the way and opened the creative doors

—E.K.R.

Grateful acknowledgment to the following people at the National Museum of
African American History and Culture for their assistance and expertise:
Lonnie G. Bunch III, Founding Director; Kinshasha Holman Conwill, Deputy Director;
Elaine Nichols, Fellowship Advisor; Tuliza Fleming, Ph.D., Curator of American Art;
Damion L. Thomas, Curator of Sports; Kassie Edwards, Research Assistant;
Jaye P. Linnen, Project Specialist; Douglas Remley, Rights & Reproductions Specialist

Special thanks to the following people at Smithsonian Enterprises:
Kealy Gordon, Product Development Manager; Jill Corcoran, Director, Licensed Publishing;
Brigid Ferraro, Vice President, Consumer and Education Products; Carol LeBlanc, President

The author and illustrator read biographies, memoirs, and online articles;
watched films and videos; listened to recordings; and visited museums, among them
the National Museum of African American History and Culture, as a part of their research.
Go to cherylwillishudson.com/resources for a list of their sources.

Contents

Ruby Bridges

BORN: SEPTEMBER 8, 1954, TYLERTOWN, MS

Kids know nothing about racism.
They're taught that by adults.

When Ruby Bridges walked up the steps of William Frantz Elementary School on her first day of school, she had to pass through a mob of protesting, screaming adults. It was November 14, 1960, and these hateful whites didn't want a six-year-old Black child attending school with their children. To protect her, four United States marshals escorted Ruby to class. Legendary artist Norman Rockwell commemorated Ruby's experience in his famous painting *The Problem We All Live With*. That image, however, did not capture the full scale of the trauma Ruby experienced.

Ruby was born into a loving family of poor sharecroppers who had moved to New Orleans, determined to make a better life for their children. When Ruby became the first child to desegregate a formerly all-white school in the South, her father lost his job and her grandparents were evicted from their farm. But Ruby was courageous and undaunted. She attended school every day, even though she was the only student in her class and wasn't allowed to play with the white students at recess.

Eventually, the public schools in New Orleans were desegregated and Ruby graduated from an integrated high school. She studied travel and tourism and became a travel agent. In the early 1990s, Ruby volunteered as a parent liaison at the elementary school that had once ostracized her.

Ruby, now Ruby Bridges Hall and the mother of four adult sons, still lives in New Orleans, where she chairs the Ruby Bridges Foundation, formed in 1999 to promote "the values of tolerance, respect, and appreciation of all differences." In 2001, President Bill Clinton awarded her the Presidential Citizens Medal. Her inspiring life was documented in the children's book *The Story of Ruby Bridges,* and in the Disney TV movie of the same name. Ruby told her own story in the children's book *Through My Eyes.* In her adult life, Ruby continues to demonstrate the courage and commitment that helped her integrate the public schools in New Orleans.

Marian Anderson

BORN: FEBRUARY 27, 1897, PHILADELPHIA, PA
DIED: APRIL 8, 1993, PORTLAND, OR

None of us is responsible for the complexion of his skin. This fact of nature offers no clue to the character or quality of the person underneath.

On an Easter Sunday morning in 1939, Marian Anderson, the internationally acclaimed contralto, sang on the steps of the Lincoln Memorial to a welcoming crowd of over 75,000 people, and to millions more who heard her beautiful voice over the radio. Earlier, she had been denied permission to hold the concert in Constitution Hall, which was owned by the Daughters of the American Revolution. Outraged by this racist affront, First Lady Eleanor Roosevelt resigned her membership in the organization and, along with others, made arrangements for Marian to sing at the Lincoln Memorial. Marian was already famous, but this highly publicized performance gave her even greater prominence on the national and international stage. It also focused more public attention on institutionalized racism in the United States.

Marian had always loved to sing. From age six, she sang in the Union Baptist Church choir in Philadelphia. Although her family and teachers recognized and encouraged her tremendous talent, Marian's parents could not afford to give her music lessons. Her father did buy a piano, however, and Marian taught herself how to play. When she was twelve, members of her church raised money to pay for private voice lessons with Giuseppe Boghetti, a famous teacher. After only two years of study, Marian was performing all over the city and entering national music competitions. At age twenty-eight, she won a competition organized by the New York Philharmonic Society, and more opportunities soon followed.

Marian had a stellar international career, and she thrilled audiences when performing the works of classical Western composers and African American spirituals. She also broke down many racial barriers. She sang at the White House for President Franklin D. Roosevelt, and in 1955, she became the first African American to perform at the New York Metropolitan Opera, as Ulrica in Verdi's *Un Ballo in Maschera*.

Marian sang at the inaugurations of presidents Dwight D. Eisenhower and John F. Kennedy and served as a delegate to the United Nations. She was awarded the Presidential Medal of Freedom by President Kennedy in 1963 and received numerous honors for her lifetime of achievements.

Althea Gibson

BORN: AUGUST 25, 1927, SILVER, SC
DIED: SEPTEMBER 28, 2003, EAST ORANGE, NJ

The loser says it may be possible, but it's difficult; the winner says it may be difficult, but it's possible.

Althea Gibson was a phenomenal tennis player and professional golfer who broke international barriers. She was the first person of color to win a Grand Slam title, at the 1956 French Open, and became the first African American to win the Wimbledon tennis tournament in 1957, winning straight sets, 6–3 6–2, in less than an hour. Althea's Wimbledon performance so impressed Queen Elizabeth II of England that the queen personally shook her hand, congratulating the champion. She also became the first African American to win the US Open (then called the US Nationals) that year. Althea continued to break records in 1958 when she won the US Open and Wimbledon for the second time.

As a child, Althea and her family moved during the Great Migration to Harlem, in New York City, where she played paddle tennis on the street. She often skipped school to practice, despite her parents' objections. A local musician, Buddy Walker, spotted Althea's talent and introduced her to tennis at the Harlem River Tennis Club. Later, neighbors helped finance her lessons at the Cosmopolitan Tennis Club.

Althea's entry to amateur tennis was fraught with prejudice and often compared to Jackie Robinson's acceptance into professional baseball. Under the mentorship and sponsorship of legendary Doc Walter Johnson and Dr. Hubert Eaton, Althea received advanced instruction within the segregated American Tennis Association. In 1949, Althea became the first African American woman to play in the USTA National Indoor Championship. One year later she became the first African American invited to play in the US Nationals at Forest Hills. Althea continued to break barriers and records during her lifetime by winning eleven Grand Slam tournaments and more than fifty-six national and international singles and doubles titles by 1958.

Althea achieved many other firsts as a musician, a professional golfer, and a recreation and sports commissioner in New Jersey. She mentored younger athletes through neighborhood and urban tennis clinics, was inducted into the International Women's Sports Hall of Fame, and was an inspiration to tennis players who followed her, including Arthur Ashe, Leslie Allen, Zina Garrison, and Venus and Serena Williams, who said, "Althea Gibson paved the way for all women of color in sport."

Toni Morrison

BORN: FEBRUARY 18, 1931, LORAIN, OH | **DIED:** AUGUST 5, 2019, NEW YORK, NY

If there is a book that you want to read, but it hasn't been written yet, you must be the one to write it.

Toni Morrison was the first Black woman to be awarded the Nobel Prize in Literature. Her novels *The Bluest Eye, Song of Solomon,* and *Beloved* are among her most famous and critically acclaimed works. Toni's career encompassed teaching English literature, editing, literary criticism, playwriting, and public speaking. Her extraordinary writing earned her international awards and honors including the Pulitzer Prize, the National Book Award, the National Humanities Medal, the PEN/Saul Bellow Award for Achievement in American Fiction, and the Presidential Medal of Freedom.

Born to working-class parents in an Ohio steel industry town, Toni's birth name was Chloe Ardelia Wofford, but she took the baptismal name Anthony after converting to Catholicism at age twelve. Later she adopted the nickname Toni. Storytelling, singing, sharing history and folklore, and telling ghost stories were central to Wofford family life. Toni drew upon this legacy and her family's love of Black culture in her epic, mythic, and richly textured novels.

Following her graduation from Howard University in 1953, Toni taught at several colleges, divorced her husband, and raised their two sons as a single mother. She joined a writer's group, then became a fiction editor at Random House, where she worked for eighteen years, co-editing with Middleton A. Harris the seminal work *The Black Book* in 1974 and editing memoirs by Muhammad Ali, Lucille Clifton, and Angela Davis. Her first novel, *The Bluest Eye,* about the ravages of slavery on an African American family, was published when she was thirty-nine years old.

Beloved, based on the true story of ex-slave Margaret Garner, was published in 1988 and won the Pulitzer Prize. It was an Oprah Winfrey Book Club selection and was later made into a movie starring Oprah and Danny Glover.

A *Paris Review* interview described Toni as "a master of the public novel, examining the relationships between races and sexes and the struggle between civilization and nature, while at the same time combining myth and the fantastic with a deep political sensitivity."

Michelle Obama

BORN: JANUARY 17, 1964, CHICAGO, IL

**I never cut class. I loved getting A's, I liked being smart.
I liked being on time. I thought being smart is cooler
than anything in the world.**

Michelle Obama, the first African American First Lady, is a unique combination of self-assurance, intelligence, organizational leadership, and style that comforts and inspires. As First Lady and wife of Barack Obama, the forty-fourth president of the United States, Michelle embraced issues of women's empowerment and community involvement. Since leaving the White House, Michelle has assured the American public that she is still "becoming," despite already being one of the most influential and successful women in the world.

Given her high-powered but nonpaying job as First Lady, Michelle initially described herself as "mom-in-chief." During her eight years in the White House, she advocated for military families, reactivated a White House kitchen garden, promoted healthy eating for schoolchildren, and started a Let's Move! physical fitness initiative. She also reaffirmed the White House's commitment to the arts and maintained a joint policy with President Obama of opening the doors of the People's House to as many visitors as possible.

Michelle was born on the South Side of Chicago, Illinois, to working-class parents Fraser and Marian Robinson. She excelled in academics, eventually following her brother, Craig, to Princeton University, before attending Harvard Law School. While working for a Chicago corporate law firm, she mentored Barack Obama, a law school associate. The couple married in 1992 and have two daughters, Malia and Sasha.

Michelle has often said, "Success isn't about how much money you make; it's about the difference you make in people's lives." After leaving corporate law, Michelle worked for Public Allies, a nonprofit organization; the University of Chicago; and the University of Chicago Medical Center. Although initially wary of politics, Michelle campaigned for her husband's run for Illinois state senate in 1996 and the US Senate in 2004, and his successful presidential campaigns in 2008 and 2012.

About her bestselling memoir *Becoming,* Michelle tweeted, "I hope my journey inspires readers to find the courage to become whoever they aspire to be."

Sojourner Truth

BORN: C. 1797, SWARTEKILL, NY | **DIED:** NOVEMBER 26, 1883, BATTLE CREEK, MI

And the Lord gave me the name Truth, because I was to declare the truth to the people.

Sojourner Truth, an abolitionist, evangelist, and women's rights activist, was born into slavery around 1797 in Dutch-speaking Upstate New York and named Isabella (Belle) Baumfree. She experienced the pains, indignities, and violence of slavery from at least four masters before escaping from bondage with her infant daughter, Sophia, and living with a nearby abolitionist family. The Van Wageners bought her freedom for twenty dollars and later helped Isabella sue for the return of her five-year-old son, Peter, who had been illegally sold into slavery in Alabama. Isabella was the first Black woman to sue a white man in a United States court and win.

One year after slavery was officially outlawed in New York, Isabella moved to New York City and worked for a minister and his family. She eventually joined several religious communities, including the Methodist Perfectionists. In 1843, after a spiritual awakening, Isabella changed her name to Sojourner Truth. Now a devout Christian, she acknowledged a call by the Spirit to embark on a journey preaching the gospel and speaking out against slavery and in favor of women's rights. Although Sojourner never learned to read or write, she was a powerful and charismatic orator, "testifying the hope that was in her."

In *The Narrative of Sojourner Truth,* which was dictated to Olive Gilbert in 1850, Sojourner recalls being sold at auction around the age of nine along with a flock of sheep. This debasement, among other violent treatments while in bondage, convinced Sojourner to evangelize against the sins of slavery. Her testimonials and book and photograph sales supported her lecture tours around the country. She would meet other abolitionists, such as Frederick Douglass, William Lloyd Garrison, and Harriet Beecher Stowe.

Standing almost six feet tall, Sojourner stirred audiences with her radical sermons. During the Civil War, she petitioned for the acceptance of Black soldiers in the Union Army and met with President Abraham Lincoln at the White House.

After the war, Sojourner worked on behalf of the Freedmen's Bureau in Washington, DC. For the rest of her life, she crusaded for human rights, reform of the prison system, and land resettlement for freed Blacks and the Exodus Movement to Kansas.

Bessie Coleman

BORN: JANUARY 26, 1892, ATLANTA, TX | **DIED:** APRIL 30, 1926, JACKSONVILLE, FL

The air is the only place free from prejudices.

On Labor Day, September 3, 1922, a pretty, petite, uniformed aviator climbed into an airplane at Curtiss Airfield in Garden City on Long Island, New York. She was ready to perform in an air show for an audience of thousands of men and women. They had come to watch her do airplane stunts of figure eights, loop the loops, barrels, and flips high above them in the sky. She did not disappoint the crowd. The barnstorming pilot was thirty-year-old Elizabeth "Bessie" Coleman, who changed the face of aviation in America.

"Queen Bess," as the press called her, was a determined young woman who had grown up in poverty in Texas, the tenth of thirteen children. She attended a one-room school four miles from her home in Waxahachie. She became an avid reader, intrigued by news of the Wright brothers' 1903 flight in Kitty Hawk, North Carolina. After years of doing laundry and picking cotton, Bessie was determined to make something better out of her life, so in 1915 she moved to Chicago to live with two of her brothers. She dreamed of learning to fly a plane.

One of Bessie's brothers was a veteran of World War I, and he often shared stories of the bold and adventurous exploits of the female French pilots he met during his military service. Bess saved the money she earned as a manicurist and taught herself French so she could study aviation abroad.

Bessie made her dreams known in her community and, encouraged by Robert Abbott, the owner of the *Chicago Defender* newspaper, she headed to France. After completing a seven-month course, Bessie became the first woman of Black and Native heritage to receive an international pilot's license from a French aviation school on June 15, 1921. Along the way she had become a media phenomenon.

In spite of rampant racism and sexism and the inherent dangers of stunt flying, for five more years Bessie barnstormed, flew, parachuted, and lectured about her experiences to Black and white audiences. A brilliant self-promoter, Bessie bought a plane of her own with the dream of one day opening an aviation school for African Americans.

Bessie fell to her death from a plane 3,000 feet in the air in Jacksonville, Florida. But her incredible accomplishments against incredible odds have inspired generations of women and African Americans to pursue *their* dreams.

Nina Simone

BORN: FEBRUARY 21, 1933, TRYON, NC
DIED: APRIL 21, 2003, CARRY-LE-ROUET, FRANCE

I'm a real rebel with a cause.

Nina Simone was a songwriter and activist dubbed the High Priestess of Soul. Her repertoire was a unique blend of jazz, blues, soul, R & B, and gospel, influenced by her training as a classical pianist. Throughout her career, Nina was celebrated as a master griot, or storyteller, who hypnotized her audiences with her interpretation of lyrics and her musicianship. Her autobiography and one of her most popular albums were titled *I Put a Spell on You.*

She was born Eunice Kathleen Waymon to strict but loving parents. Nina loved music and could play the piano by ear when she was only three years old. She took lessons from a classically trained white pianist, graduated as valedictorian of her high school class, and with financial help from people in her community, enrolled in the Juilliard School of Music. Later, she was denied admission to the Curtis Institute of Music in Philadelphia due to racial discrimination. To hide her career as a pianist and singer in jazz clubs from her parents, she changed her name to Nina Simone. She was able to earn enough money from her act to pay for private lessons. By the time she was twenty-five years old, Nina had attracted a solid following and signed a record contract with Bethlehem Records.

Between 1958 and 1993, Nina made more than sixty albums, consistently taking musical risks in live and studio performances. Using her distinct contralto voice, she also gained a reputation as an edgy, defiant, and uncompromising artist. During the 1960s, influenced by friends Lorraine Hansberry, James Baldwin, and Langston Hughes, Nina increasingly saw her music as a vehicle for social change. Compositions such as "I Wish I Knew How It Would Feel to Be Free," "Four Women," and "To Be Young, Gifted, and Black" reflected this commitment.

Nina lived abroad for much of her life after the 1970s, disillusioned with being underappreciated as a musician in the United States. Following her death in France, Nina's birthplace was designated a National Treasure by the National Trust for Historic Preservation in 2018. She was posthumously inducted into the Rock & Roll Hall of Fame.

Ida B. Wells

BORN: JULY 16, 1862, HOLLY SPRINGS, MS | **DIED:** MARCH 25, 1931, CHICAGO, IL

The way to right wrongs is to turn the light of truth upon them.

Ida B. Wells was an American investigative journalist, feminist, and militant activist who for decades led an anti-lynching crusade in the United States. Ida was also a fiery public speaker, a community organizer, and an advocate for social justice. She traveled throughout the South gathering data about lynchings and eventually published the statistics in her 1895 pamphlet, *A Red Record*.

Ida was born into slavery in 1862. Her parents, James and Lizzie Wells, were active in local Republican politics during the period of Reconstruction, and Ida attended Rust University, a school for newly freed slaves, where her father served on the board of trustees. The oldest of seven siblings, Ida dropped out of school to raise the others.

Ida later taught in Mississippi and then Memphis, Tennessee. While traveling between Memphis and Nashville, she was illegally ejected from her first-class seat on the train after she refused to move to a smoking car set aside for Blacks. Ida fought and won an 1884 lawsuit against the Chesapeake and Ohio Railroad, but the judgment was overturned by the Tennessee Supreme Court. Always outspoken about injustice, Ida was fired from her teaching position in Memphis's segregated schools when she wrote about unequal teacher salaries.

Using the pen name Iola, Ida wrote articles and editorials in a number of church-related publications including *The Living Way* and *The Evening Star*. In 1889, she became a co-owner of *Free Speech and Headlight*, an anti-segregation newspaper in Tennessee. After three of her friends were lynched by a Memphis mob, Ida began documenting lynchings nationwide.

Ida left Memphis and moved to Chicago in 1892 after her press was destroyed and her life was threatened by white vigilantes, but she continued to write articles for such Black newspapers as the *New York Age* and the *Chicago Conservator*. In 1893, she married attorney and newspaper editor Ferdinand Lee Barnett and began raising their four children while traveling, lecturing, and organizing civic organizations to address women's rights and civil rights. She founded the National Association of Colored Women's Clubs and a number of other clubs and organizations, and was a founding member of the Niagara Movement, a precursor of the NAACP.

Barbara Jordan

BORN: FEBRUARY 21, 1936, HOUSTON, TX | **DIED:** JANUARY 17, 1996, AUSTIN, TX

Justice of right is always to take precedence over might.

Barbara Jordan raised her arms to quiet the thunderous applause greeting her in Madison Square Garden. It was July 1976, and as representative from the 18th District in Texas, the congresswoman took her place at the podium to begin her keynote address at the Democratic National Convention. She was the first African American elected to the Texas state senate after Reconstruction, and the first African American woman elected to the United States House of Representatives. Barbara was also an experienced, seasoned educator and orator, who had been a champion debater in high school and college. When she spoke, people listened.

Barbara was the youngest of three daughters born to Benjamin Jordan and Arlyne Patten. She majored in political science and history at Texas Southern University before earning her law degree from Boston University in 1959. Known for her compelling voice and intellect, Barbara returned to Houston to start a private law practice, but she was soon in the political arena, first participating in the 1960 Kennedy-Johnson campaign, then starting her own political career in 1966. In 1972, she was elected to the United States House of Representatives.

While serving on the House Judiciary Committee during the Watergate hearings in July 1974, Barbara quoted the original drafters of the Constitution in a televised speech, "Statements on the Articles of Impeachment," in support of President Richard Nixon's impeachment and in defense of the American system of checks and balances. Her speech is often considered one of the best of the twentieth century: "I am not going to sit here and be an idle spectator to the diminution, the subversion, the destruction of the Constitution."

During her tenure as a congresswoman, Representative Jordan sponsored or cosponsored more than three hundred bills and resolutions. She was a staunch supporter of civil rights and banking reform, and was known for her high ethical standards.

Among Barbara's numerous awards and honors are the 1992 Spingarn Medal from the NAACP, the 1994 Presidential Medal of Freedom, and her induction in 1990 to the National Women's Hall of Fame in Seneca Falls, New York.

Aretha Franklin

BORN: MARCH 25, 1942, MEMPHIS, TN | DIED: AUGUST 16, 2018, DETROIT, MI

**Being a singer is a natural gift.
It means I'm using to the highest degree
possible the gift that God gave me to use.**

Aretha Franklin rose from the piano during a 2015 Kennedy Center performance of "A Natural Woman." Midway through the vocals, she picked up a handheld mic and dropped her floor-length mink coat. The audience leapt to its feet in a spontaneous standing ovation. They were paying homage to the Queen of Soul.

Aretha was raised in Detroit, where her father, the dynamic, nationally recognized preacher Rev. C. L. Franklin, was the pastor of New Bethel Baptist Church. Aretha taught herself to play the piano by ear and began singing in church by age nine. Billed as "Lil' Aretha" on her father's preaching tours, fourteen-year-old Aretha developed her skills as a singer and musician. She also found inspiration from the African American recording artists who often visited her father, including Mahalia Jackson, Clara Ward, James Cleveland, Sam Cook, and Jackie Wilson.

After recording a number of singles and albums, Aretha became a breakout star in 1967 when her new label, Atlantic Records, allowed her to release an album that incorporated her gospel background and her own creativity. That year alone, Aretha released the hits "Baby I Love You," "Do Right Woman, Do Right Man," "A Natural Woman," "I Never Loved a Man," and "Respect," which became her signature song and an anthem for the civil rights and women's movements.

One of the bestselling musical artists and singers of all time, Aretha won eighteen Grammys and was inducted into the Rock and Roll Hall of Fame and the Gospel Music Hall of Fame. She sang at the funeral of Dr. Martin Luther King Jr. in 1968 and was awarded the Presidential Medal of Freedom in 2005. Four years later, she sang at the 2009 inauguration of President Barack Obama.

Aretha died from pancreatic cancer in 2018, at age seventy-six. President and Mrs. Obama shared their sense of loss, but also their profound admiration for Aretha's genius: "Aretha helped define the American experience. In her voice, we could feel our history, all of it and in every shade—our power and our pain, our darkness and our light, our quest for redemption and our hard-won respect. She helped us feel more connected to each other, more hopeful, more human."

Mary McLeod Bethune

BORN: JULY 10, 1875, MAYESVILLE, SC | **DIED:** MAY 18, 1955, DAYTONA BEACH, FL

**I leave you finally a responsibility
to our young people. . . .
Our children must never lose their
zeal for building a better world.**

In 1904, Mary McLeod Bethune rented a cottage in Daytona Beach, Florida, filling it with cast-off furniture and makeshift supplies. This determined educator started her own school for girls when many areas of the country had no schools for African Americans, especially girls. At first, Mary and her students sold sweet potato pies and solicited donations from area businesses, churches, and clubs to help fund her school. Encouraged by fellow educator Booker T. Washington, she reached out to such national figures as John D. Rockefeller, who donated generously. Armed with dogged determination, incredible organizational skills, and unwavering faith, Mary guided her students and faculty as her school grew. In 1923, it merged with the Cookman Institute, and in 1931 was named Bethune-Cookman College in recognition of Mary's leadership and direction. Today, Bethune Cookman University is a highly regarded historically Black college and university (HBCU).

The fifteenth child of former slaves, Mary was born in 1875 on a farm near Mayesville, South Carolina. When she was ten, she enrolled in a one-room school, where she learned to read. Later she attended Scotia Seminary in North Carolina and the Moody Bible Institute in Chicago. Mary taught at a number of schools, including the Haines Institute for African Americans in Augusta, Georgia, founded by pioneering educator Lucy Craft Laney, who inspired Mary to follow in her footsteps.

As her school grew, Mary became a national leader on issues related to civil rights, education, women, and young people. She served as president of the prestigious National Association of Colored Women's Clubs and founded the National Council of Negro Women. She organized the fight against school segregation and inadequate healthcare for Black children with the support of the Women's Clubs. As the director of Negro affairs at the National Youth Administration, a federal agency, she was the highest-ranking African American woman in government during the administration of President Franklin D. Roosevelt. From humble beginnings, Mary became one of the most powerful and influential African Americans in the United States.

Katherine Johnson

BORN: AUGUST 26, 1918, WHITE SULPHUR SPRINGS, WV
DIED: FEBRUARY 24, 2020, NEWPORT NEWS, VA

We needed to be assertive as women. In those days, assertive and aggressive—and the degree to which we had to be that way—depended on where you were. I had to be.

Katherine Johnson was a pioneering research mathematician at NASA best known for her accuracy in computerized celestial navigation. She calculated the trajectories for the May 5, 1961, flight of Alan Shepard Jr., the first American in space, and her calculations were critical to the success of the 1969 Apollo 11 flight to the moon, the beginnings of the space shuttle program, and beyond.

Katherine was a curious child who loved to ask questions. From an early age, she showed an aptitude for mathematics. She was admitted to high school at age ten, graduated at age fourteen, and became the first African American woman to attend graduate school at West Virginia University.

In 1952, after a successful teaching career and raising a family, Katherine applied to the National Advisory Committee for Aeronautics for a job as a human "computer." At this precursor to NASA, she did calculations for Langley's Guidance and Navigation Department, analyzing such topics as gust alleviation for aircraft. The author of more than twenty-five papers, she fought for the right to participate in editorial review meetings, which no woman had previously attended. Astronaut John Glenn relied on her calculations before embarking on his historic mission orbiting the Earth.

Initially assigned to the colored computer pool supervised by Dorothy Vaughan, Katherine made a successful transition from calculating complex equations with a pencil to working with mainframe digital computers to computing guidance systems for the space shuttle.

Katherine experienced years of Jim Crow segregation and gender discrimination as a woman working in an industry dominated by white male engineers. In 2015, she received the Presidential Medal of Freedom. Her life was featured in *Hidden Figures,* an acclaimed film based on the book of the same title by Margot Lee Shetterly, and the Katherine G. Johnson Computational Research Facility was formally dedicated at Langley Research Center in Hampton, Virginia, in 2016.

Shirley Chisholm

BORN: NOVEMBER 30, 1924, BROOKLYN, NY
DIED: JANUARY 1, 2005, ORMOND BEACH, FL

You don't make progress by standing on the sidelines, whimpering and complaining. You make progress by implementing ideas.

Throughout her life, Shirley Anita St. Hill Chisholm was keenly aware of the dual obstacles of being Black and a woman. But those obstacles never stopped her. In 1968, she became the first Black woman elected to the United States Congress, and in 1972, she was the first to run for the highest office in the land when she sought the Democratic nomination for president of the United States.

Shirley's mother was a seamstress in Barbados, and her father was a domestic worker in Guyana. They both immigrated to Brooklyn, where they raised four daughters. Shirley, the oldest, was an excellent student and won prizes for her debate skills at Brooklyn College. While studying for her master's degree, she taught in a nursery school. Later, she became a director of daycare centers in Brooklyn and lower Manhattan, where she developed a keen understanding of child welfare and early-education issues. Advocating for children led Shirley to the world of politics. She worked with the League of Women Voters, the Urban League, and the Democratic Party. In 1964, she was elected to the New York General Assembly, and in 1968, she launched a campaign for the United States House of Representatives to represent Brooklyn's 12th Congressional District. Shirley served until 1983. While there, she championed bills for equal employment opportunities, built alliances with women's groups and people of color, fought for improved services for women and children, and protested the country's involvement in the Vietnam War.

Shirley's determined spirit paved the way for others, including women and minorities. When she died in 2005, she left a tremendous legacy of educational and governmental service. In November 2015, she was posthumously awarded the Presidential Medal of Freedom by President Barack Obama. Shirley's campaign slogan when she ran for president, "Unbought and Unbossed," aptly described the woman known to many as Fighting Shirley.

Lena Horne

BORN: JUNE 30, 1917, BROOKLYN, NY | DIED: MAY 9, 2010, NEW YORK, NY

I don't have to be a symbol to anybody, I don't have to be a first to anybody. . . . I'm me, and I'm like nobody else.

From the time she was two years old, Lena Horne made headlines. In 1919, she appeared on the cover of a print advertisement for the NAACP's *Crisis Magazine,* as part of the organization's appeal to increase membership and support for their social justice programs. Fourteen years later, she debuted as a chorus girl dancer at the Cotton Club in Harlem, in New York City. She became a successful nightclub performer before moving to Hollywood, where she broke new ground when she signed a seven-year contract with MGM, a major motion picture studio. Lena had a glamorous yet controversial career. She challenged racial barriers in an industry that capitalized on her talents while denying her many opportunities.

In Hollywood, Lena courageously refused to act in roles that were demeaning to Blacks. But many of her scenes were edited out of the films when shown to segregated white audiences. Lena became famous for her starring roles in the 1943 films *Cabin in the Sky* and *Stormy Weather,* but she was blacklisted in Hollywood in the 1950s because of her political activities and the fear of Communism. Nevertheless, Lena earned admittance into Hollywood's prestigious Screen Actors Guild, becoming one of the first Black women to do so.

Disillusioned with Hollywood, Lena returned to New York and established a triumphant career as one of the premier nightclub performers of the post-war era. In 1958, she was nominated for a Tony Award and she became a bestselling recording artist. *Lena Horne: The Lady and Her Music* had a spectacular 333-performace run on Broadway. In 1989, she received the Grammy's Lifetime Achievement Award.

During her seventy-year career in entertainment, Lena was always involved in civil rights causes. From anti-lynching campaigns supported by Eleanor Roosevelt in the 1930s and 1940s to voter registration drives in the 1960s and 1970s, she spoke on behalf of the NAACP, SNCC, CORE, and the National Council of Negro Women. She participated with Harry Belafonte and other entertainers in the 1963 March on Washington and at rallies to support murdered civil rights worker Medgar Evers. Among her most cherished awards was the 1983 Spingarn Medal given by the NAACP, the organization that first promoted her career in 1919.

Wilma Rudolph

BORN: JUNE 23, 1940, SAINT BETHLEHEM, TN
DIED: NOVEMBER 12, 1994, BRENTWOOD, TN

We are all the same in this notion:
The potential for greatness lives within each of us.

Wilma Rudolph was four years old when she was stricken with polio. Doctors said she would not walk again. But Wilma's mother took her daughter to weekly therapy, and she and her other children massaged Wilma's legs every day. By age eight, Wilma could walk with the aid of a brace. A few years later, she was playing basketball with her brothers. At age sixteen, Wilma competed as a sprinter in the 1956 Olympic Games. In 1960, when she competed in the Rome Olympics, most people were not aware of Wilma's story of triumph over adversity. To them she was just another athlete. But when she became the first woman to win three gold medals in track, she received international recognition and was named "athlete of the year" by the Associated Press.

Wilma Glodean Rudolph, the twentieth of twenty-two siblings, was raised in Tennessee. She set a state record for high school girls' basketball by scoring 803 points as a sophomore. While playing in a game, she was spotted by Ed Temple, coach of the Tennessee State University track and field team. He recognized her natural athletic ability and invited her to train with his team, called the Tigerbelles. At the 1960 Rome Olympics, the first to be televised internationally, Wilma was the fastest woman runner in the world.

When Wilma returned home, her town wanted to honor her with a parade. Most of the city facilities were still segregated, but Wilma insisted that any banquet or parade for her had to be fully integrated. The city planners complied. After retiring from competitive sports in 1963, Wilma went back to school to study elementary education. She taught in public schools and colleges and continued to use her celebrity status and skills to support civil rights causes. She coached and mentored young women and athletes of color and established the Wilma Rudolph Foundation in Indianapolis, a community-based amateur sports program that she considered her greatest success.

Faith Ringgold

BORN: OCTOBER 8, 1930, HARLEM, NEW YORK, NY

My process is designed to give us "colored folk" and women a taste of the American dream straight up.

Faith Ringgold describes herself as a painter, a sculptor, an art activist, a feminist, and an educator. She broke ground during the 1960s and 1970s in the world of contemporary fine art when her protests and performance events took center stage in the New York museum art world. Now renowned for her story quilts, Faith is also the author-illustrator of more than a dozen children's books, including the Caldecott Honor Book *Tar Beach*. Central to her work of six decades are social commentary; an interest in African rhythm, pattern, color, and repetition; and embracing what she calls an authentic "Black aesthetic."

Faith was the youngest of three children born and raised in Harlem during the Great Depression to Willi Posey Jones and Andrew Louis Jones. Faith's mother was a fashion designer and encouraged her early interest in art and taught her how to sew. Her father was an avid reader and storyteller, and their home was always filled with musicians, artists, writers, and creative performers from the vibrant Harlem arts scene.

When Faith enrolled at the City College of New York in 1950, she studied art education instead of majoring in art due to the college's sexist curriculum policy. She began teaching art in the New York public school system but became increasingly interested in pursuing a career in painting, inspired by her friends James Baldwin, Jacob Lawrence, and Amiri Baraka.

In her memoir, *We Flew Over the Bridge*, Faith recounts transformative moments in her search for recognition as a painter and how they grew out of everyday life experiences, the intersection of her involvement in the civil rights movement of the 1960s, her confrontation of systematic and institutional racism in the 1970s and '80s, and her personal experience with blatant sexual bias in the arts throughout her career.

Faith's story quilts capture a wide range of experiences through a unique combination of fantasy, realism, written narration, figurative expression, African American history, social commentary, and activism. Her work is collected by major museums worldwide, including the Metropolitan Museum of Art, the Guggenheim Museum, the Museum of Modern Art, and the National Museum of African American History and Culture.

Madam C. J. Walker

BORN: DECEMBER 23, 1867, DELTA, LA | DIED: MAY 25, 1919, IRVINGTON, NY

I got my start by giving myself a start.

Madam C. J. Walker, born Sarah Breedlove, is an iconic figure in African American history because of her success as a businesswoman, philanthropist, and political activist. Against tremendous odds, including a lack of formal education, she created an eponymous empire of hair-care products and services and a national sales force, which during her lifetime became a model of entrepreneurship and leadership for African Americans. She's often referred to as the first self-made Black female millionaire in the United States.

Sarah was the first child born to Owen and Minerva Breedlove after the Emancipation Proclamation. Orphaned by age seven, she was working as a domestic three years later. After experiencing years of backbreaking work as a laundress, domestic, and cook, Sarah yearned for an educated life for her daughter and herself. In 1904, she became a commission agent, selling hair-care products for Annie Turnbo Malone at the Poro Company. Soon after, Sarah and her daughter moved to Denver, where Sarah began developing her own line of hair-care products. In 1906, she married Charles Walker, who also became her business partner. She was known as Madam C. J. Walker, a moniker that became her famous brand.

Madam Walker built a house, factory, laboratory, hair salon, and beauty school to train her sales agents. She hired women to fill key management roles within the company. At the height of her career, she employed several thousand women as sales agents, organized national conventions, and used door-to-door sales and mail-order advertising to expand her market. Her Walker Method demonstrated how women could budget, build their own businesses, and become financially independent.

She modeled civic pride and gave generously to Black colleges, benevolent organizations, and Black institutions, including the National Negro Business League, the National Association of Colored Women's Clubs, and the NAACP. She and her daughter A'Lelia also supported artists and intellectuals of the Harlem Renaissance and participated in political demonstrations to protest unfair treatment of African Americans. Two of her properties are listed on the National Register of Historic Places: Villa Lewaro in Irvington, New York, and the Madame Walker Theatre Center in Indianapolis. Her legacy continues through numerous scholarships, awards, a US postage stamp, and her induction into the National Women's Hall of Fame.

Diana Ross

BORN: MARCH 26, 1944, DETROIT, MI

You've got to get out there and make your golden dream happen for yourself.

During the early 1960s, Detroit, Michigan, became known for more than manufacturing cars. From its roots and rich Black cultural influences, a new music emerged that would become international in scope: the Motown Sound, featuring such acts as the Temptations, Smokey Robinson, the Four Tops, and the female group, the Supremes. Diana Ross, the lead singer, along with Mary Wilson and Florence Ballard, created the mega-hits "Where Did Our Love Go," "Stop! in the Name of Love," and "Come See About Me."

Diana debuted as a solo performer in 1970 with hits such as "Reach Out and Touch Somebody's Hand," mega-recording contracts, nightclub and television appearances, international concert tours, and movie roles. Diana's total hits as a solo artist and as a member of the Supremes topped seventy, and *Billboard* named her Female Entertainer of the Century. The teenage dreamer had become a glamorous diva.

Diana was born in a Detroit working-class neighborhood. She attended Cass Technical High School, studying clothing design and cosmetology with a goal of becoming a fashion designer. She dreamed big dreams and used her skills in makeup, hair care, sewing, and fashion to create a defining "look" for the Supremes. During her twenty-year contract with Motown, she performed with other Motown stars including Marvin Gaye and Lionel Richie, and was credited with discovering the Jackson 5.

After transitioning into a solo career, she became an actress and appeared in films and Broadway shows. Diana starred in *Lady Sings the Blues, Mahogany,* and *The Wiz,* and in 1974, she was the first African American female to co-host the Academy Awards. In 1981, she signed a $20 million, seven-year contract with RCA, which at the time was the most expensive recording deal in history. She also owned her own production company, Anaid.

In her six-decade career, Diana has performed in high school auditoriums, TV studios, stadiums, indoor concert stages, and private venues for the queen of England, the emperor of Japan, and the president of the United States. She has donated her talents and fund-raising services to benefit international aid organizations and victims of natural disasters. She has indelibly influenced those recording artists who followed in her wake.

Augusta Fells Savage

BORN: FEBRUARY 29, 1892, GREEN COVE SPRINGS, FL
DIED: MARCH 26, 1962, NEW YORK, NY

My monument will be in (my students') work.

Augusta Fells Savage was a talented sculptor who blazed a trail as a pioneering working artist. Her activism and art helped mold and inspire the careers of future artists.

As a child, she played in the rich clay near her home. But instead of making mud pies, Augusta molded pretty figures of farm animals. Despite her minister father's objections, she continued to make sculpture. After winning a prize for her sculptures at a Florida state fair, the fair's superintendent encouraged Augusta to go to New York to study art. Armed with a letter of reference and big dreams but no formal training, Augusta enrolled at Cooper Union in 1921.

She excelled and completed her coursework in three years, but she was denied enrollment in a summer program in France because she was Black. Augusta fought back, writing a series of letters to local media, challenging the selection committee's discriminatory practices. Her story made headlines and garnered support for her work.

In 1923, she was commissioned to sculpt a portrait of W. E. B. Du Bois and later one of Marcus Garvey for the Harlem branch of the New York Public Library. In 1929, she was awarded a Rosenwald fellowship and assisted by donations raised in the Black community. Augusta attended the Académie de la Grande Chaumière, a leading art school in Paris.

Upon returning to the United States, she opened the Savage Studio of Arts and Crafts in Harlem and offered free classes and gallery space to students, who included Gwendolyn Knight, Jacob Lawrence, and Norman Lewis. In 1934, Augusta became the first African American artist to be elected to the National Association of Women Painters and Sculptors.

A huge sixteen-foot-tall harp, commissioned in 1939 for the New York World's Fair, is considered Augusta's best-known work. Inspired by the poem "Lift Every Voice and Sing" by James Weldon Johnson, its strings are a line of singing children, and the sculpture symbolizes the musical gifts of Black people.

Condoleezza Rice

BORN: NOVEMBER 14, 1954, BIRMINGHAM, AL

The essence of America, what really unites us, is not nationality or ethnicity or religion. It is an idea . . . that you can come from humble circumstances and you can do great things.

Condoleezza Rice is an accomplished educator, musician, writer, athlete, and scholar who has achieved many remarkable firsts during her lifetime. She served as the sixty-sixth Secretary of State, in the administration of President George W. Bush. She rose through the ranks of academia as a scholar specializing in Soviet studies and foreign relations and an assistant professor at Stanford University, and she was eventually appointed as the first woman, the first African American, *and* the youngest provost of that institution. Her expertise in foreign relations and fluency in Russian led her to appointments as the first female National Security Advisor and the first African American female Secretary of State.

Condoleezza was born in Birmingham, Alabama, the only child of educators Angelena Rice and Rev. John Wesley Rice. They instilled in her the belief that in spite of institutionalized racism and the Jim Crow culture that surrounded her, Condoleezza could achieve excellence. The turbulence of the Birmingham of her youth, where her playmate Denise McNair and three other young girls were killed in the 1963 bombing of the Sixteenth Street Baptist Church, greatly affected Condoleezza and her family. But she was also nurtured by a loving family and community. She began piano lessons at the age of three, she was a figure skater, and she read voraciously and achieved excellent grades. At the University of Denver, she abandoned her childhood dream of becoming a concert pianist when she discovered international studies under the mentorship of Professor Josef Korbel. Although music and competitive sports continued to be important to her, international affairs became her passion.

After receiving her PhD in political science, Condoleezza held academic and administrative positions at Stanford University. She became a highly sought after foreign policy expert. As Secretary of State, she helped to mold US policy in the Middle East, Europe, and around the world. For over thirty years, she has maintained her relationship with Stanford University, where she continues to teach.

Gwendolyn Brooks

BORN: JUNE 7, 1917, TOPEKA, KS | **DIED:** DECEMBER 3, 2000, CHICAGO, IL

What I'm fighting for now in my work . . . for an expression relevant to all manner of blacks, poems I could take into a tavern, into the street, into the halls of a housing project.

Whether Gwendolyn Brooks was standing on a stage in front of two thousand people or speaking to a public school class of twenty-five students, she captivated audiences with the power and simplicity of her exquisitely crafted words.

As a child, Gwendolyn loved to write stories and poems. Her parents encouraged her to submit her poems to magazines. At the age of thirteen, Gwendolyn's poem "Eventide" was published in *American Childhood.* By the time she was seventeen, her poems had been featured frequently in the *Chicago Defender,* a leading African American newspaper. Gwendolyn grew up on the South Side of Chicago and wrote about the lives, struggles, and celebrations of everyday people where she lived.

She was the first African American to receive the Pulitzer Prize for poetry in 1949 for *Annie Allen,* and she was nationally recognized as one of the most influential writers of the twenty-first century. A prolific writer, Gwendolyn's poetry spans classical as well as colloquial forms: ballads, sonnets, narrative, blues, and free verse. She wrote the poems in *Bronzeville Boys and Girls* for and about children.

During the 1960s and 1970s, she began publishing her work with independent Black presses such as Dudley Randall's Broadside Press and Haki Madhubuti's Third World Press. From the late 1960s, she served as a mentor to countless poets who came to prominence during the Black Arts Movement and beyond. An influential proponent of poetry workshops, Gwendolyn also offered countless poetry contests for young people, and she brought poetry to the people with readings in schools, libraries, prisons, churches, and other public venues.

Gwendolyn taught at a number of institutions, including Columbia College Chicago, Northeastern Illinois University, Chicago State University, Elmhurst College, Columbia University, and City College of New York. In 1985, at the age of 68, Gwendolyn became the first African American to serve as poetry consultant to the Library of Congress. She was also poet laureate of the state of Illinois from 1968 until her death in 2000.

Ibtihaj Muhammad

BORN: DECEMBER 4, 1985, MAPLEWOOD, NJ

**I want to be an example for minority and Muslim youth
that anything is possible with perseverance.**

Ibtihaj Muhammad, a champion Olympic fencer, is celebrated as the first American athlete to compete for the United States team while wearing the hijab, a traditional head covering. Growing up with four siblings in Maplewood, New Jersey, Ibtihaj was always active in sports, but her mother altered her uniforms so that Ibtihaj would be modestly dressed according to the tenets of her Muslim faith.

When she was thirteen, Ibtihaj discovered fencing, which allowed her to be fully covered while actively competing. It was a perfect fit. She became captain of her Columbia High School team for two years and led it to two state championships. Ibtihaj enrolled in classes at the Peter Westbrook Foundation, a nonprofit organization that teaches life skills and the sport of fencing to underprivileged youth in the New York metropolitan area. There, Ibtihaj received encouragement to pursue the sport through national and international competitions.

Despite her relatively late start, Ibtihaj's competitive fencing career has been stellar. In 2004, she earned a scholarship to Duke University and competed for the school's fencing team. After her graduation in 2007 and throughout her career, she has earned numerous medals for both team and individual events on the World Cup circuit.

Although an injury prevented her from competing in the 2012 Olympic Games, that same year she was named Muslim sportswoman of the year. In 2014, she launched a clothing line, Louella, to meet a need for comfortable, modest clothing for Muslim women. And as part of its Shero program that celebrates female achievers, Mattel Toys introduced a hijab-wearing Barbie doll in Ibtihaj's likeness.

Ibtihaj made history when she took home the bronze medal in the team sabre fencing competition at the 2016 Summer Olympic Games in Rio de Janeiro. As a sports ambassador for the State Department, she serves on the Empowering Women and Girls Through Sport Initiative. Her memoir, *Proud: My Fight for an Unlikely American Dream,* shares her story of triumph and her struggle with anxiety and how she copes with it.

Ann Lowe

BORN: DECEMBER 14, 1898, CLAYTON, AL

DIED: FEBRUARY 25, 1981, QUEENS, NEW YORK, NY

(I want) to prove that a Negro can become a major dress designer.

Ann Lowe was the first African American to be recognized as a fashion designer of haute couture. Her one-of-a-kind dresses and gowns were made of dozens of yards of satin, tulle, taffeta, and silk and were decorated with delicate embellishments of handmade flowers, intricate beadwork, and jewels. Ann created wedding, ball, and cotillion gowns for elite families, and she was best known for designing the Trapunto-styled wedding gown and attendants' dresses for the 1953 wedding of future First Lady Jacqueline Bouvier to then Senator John F. Kennedy.

Ann began sewing at the age of six. Her grandmother, an enslaved dressmaker, opened her own custom seamstress business in rural Alabama after the Civil War and continued to sew for wealthy white Southern families. When her mother died suddenly, sixteen-year-old Ann took over the family business and completed the work on several formal gowns commissioned by the governor's wife. Eventually, Ann moved to Tampa, Florida, to sew for prominent families. In 1917, she enrolled in a couture course in New York City, but due to Jim Crow practices, Ann was forced to complete her work in a separate room from the white students who objected to her presence in their class. Ann's sketches and drawings were often used by instructors as examples of the best designs of her class. She completed her course one year early.

In 1928, Ann settled in Harlem. For a time she worked on commission for stores such as Henri Bendel, Neiman Marcus, and Saks Fifth Avenue. By the 1950s, Ann's intricate and meticulous work was in such demand by society families that she opened her own salon. Many of Ann's exquisitely tailored gowns appeared in *Vogue, Vanity Fair,* and *Town & Country* magazines throughout the 1950s and '60s. Unfortunately, Ann's business consistently operated at a loss due to the high cost of materials and labor, and she did not achieve fame as a fashion designer during her lifetime. Today, however, her dresses are part of the collections of the Metropolitan Museum of Art's Costume Institute and the National Museum of African American History and Culture.

Ntozake Shange

BORN: OCTOBER 18, 1948, TRENTON, NJ | **DIED:** OCTOBER 27, 2018, BOWIE, MD

I found god in myself / and I loved her / . . . fiercely.

Poet, novelist, playwright, performance artist, and educator Ntozake Shange's unique voice and feminist approach to literature achieved widespread acclaim when her choreopoem, *for colored girls who have considered suicide when the rainbow is enuf,* was first produced on Broadway in 1975. In that production, seven nameless women dressed in colors of the rainbow spoke in twenty poems, monologues, and dance about vital issues confronted by Black women. This included themes related to artistic expression, body image, race, skin color, and male-female relationships. In the years that followed, *for colored girls* continued to be a critical success throughout the United States and Europe. It became a part of women's studies curricula and was adapted for television and film. *for colored girls* is considered a landmark and a classic in American theater. The play won an Obie Award for its off-Broadway production at the Public Theater, and it returned to the Broadway stage in 2022.

The play's phenomenal success helped to propel Ntozake's forty-plus-year career as a writer and educator. She was an award-winning author of adult novels, plays, performance pieces, and children's books, including *Sassafrass Cypress & Indigo, Ellington Was Not a Street, Float Like a Butterfly, Whitewash, We Troubled the Waters,* and *Freedom's a-Callin' Me.* She also taught and lectured at colleges and universities throughout the country.

Whether writing for adults or for children, Ntozake's works have always been informed by the literary, musical, and intellectual influences of her family experiences and the turbulent political and feminist ideologies of the 1960s and '70s. Born in New Jersey, she was named Paulette Linda Williams. Her parents' friends included a host of notable African American and Latinx influencers. In 1971, she changed what she considered a slave name to Ntozake Shange, which in Xhosa and Zulu means "she who comes with her own things and walks like a lion." Ntozake continued to embrace cultural influences from the African diaspora in her literary works, while teaching and working as a performance artist in California.

Ntozake struggled with undiagnosed bipolar disorder during her young adulthood and beyond. After a series of strokes and an autoimmune disease, she resumed her writing career, publishing her last volume of poetry, *Wild Beauty,* in 2015.

Carla Hayden

BORN: AUGUST 10, 1952, TALLAHASSEE, FL

Librarians are a cornerstone of democracy—
where information is free and equally available to everyone.

Carla Hayden stepped alongside four-year-old Daliyah Marie Arana and congratulated her on reading more than a thousand books. As she encouraged Daliyah, the 2017 Library of Congress "Librarian for a Day," Carla reflected on her own journey as a historian, a public children's librarian, a college professor, the CEO of the Baltimore library system, and the fourteenth United States Librarian of Congress, the first woman and the first African American to serve in this prestigious position, and the first professionally trained librarian to be appointed to lead the Library of Congress in over sixty years.

Carla calls herself the "accidental librarian," because she took what she thought was a temporary job at a small storefront branch library in Chicago. After graduate studies at the University of Chicago, Carla earned influential positions at several leading libraries, including the Chicago Public Library, where she first met Barack and Michelle Obama; the University of Pittsburgh, where she served as an assistant professor for Library and Information Science; the Enoch Pratt Free Library in Baltimore, Maryland, where she was named only the second African American CEO; and, finally, achieved the position of librarian-in-chief, overseeing the entire operation of the Library of Congress, with more than 3,149 full-time employees, 838 miles of shelving, and 167 million volumes of books, manuscripts, photos, maps, sheet music, recordings, and book-related items. She is the leader of the nation's and the world's largest library.

She often mentions her favorite childhood book, *Bright April,* written by Marguerite de Angeli in 1946, about a young African American Brownie scout who turns a racist encounter into an opportunity for friendship. It meant so much for Carla to read a book about a girl who looked like her. Carla's early passion for reading would later develop into a mission for libraries to serve as gateways to information and to keep libraries relevant by using technology to make books accessible to the widest possible audience of readers. The first Librarian of Congress to use Twitter, Carla is actively involved in creating the "libraries of the future" by utilizing strategic digital planning, online engagement, podcasts, increased digital access to special collections, live-streaming, mobile apps, and programs such as Ask a Librarian.

Sheryl Swoopes

BORN: MARCH 25, 1971, BROWNFIELD, TX

At times, I get it in my mind that there is no way I can miss.

Sheryl Swoopes was the first player to be signed to the Women's National Basketball Association (WNBA) in 1997. Recruited by the Houston Comets, she joined the team only six weeks after giving birth to her son, playing the last third of the initial season and leading her team to the championship. During her WNBA career, Sheryl was a four-time champion and a three-time MVP selection. In 2011, she was named one of the league's top fifteen players of all time.

During her professional career, Sheryl, who stands six feet tall, displayed such athleticism and formidable hoop skills that she was often referred to as Her Airness. Her legendary career helped stabilize the WNBA as a popular professional sport. Players in the WNBA don't receive big salaries like NBA players. Many played for international teams during the off-season to augment their WNBA incomes. So did Sheryl.

Sheryl was the first female athlete to secure a major shoe sponsorship when Nike introduced her brand, Air Swoopes. She also won three Olympic gold medals as a member of the United States national team in 1996, 2000, and 2004. In 2005, Sheryl became the highest-profile team sport athlete to come out publicly as a lesbian.

Sheryl grew up in Brownfield, Texas, with her mother, Louise Swoopes, who was divorced. Sheryl started playing organized basketball at the age of seven, but she also shot hoops with her three brothers and developed her famous skills while competing with them. Sheryl was recruited by the University of Texas, transferred to South Plains College, then played for Texas Tech University as a Lady Raider. Sheryl was the only player, male or female, to score forty-seven points in a collegiate national championship game. Her moves on the court were electrifying. Even the sound of her last name, Swoopes, evoked the basketball lexicon, combining *swish* and *hoops*.

After retiring from active play in 2011, Sheryl became a college basketball coach. She was inducted into the Naismith Memorial Basketball Hall of Fame in 2016 and the Houston Sports Hall of Fame in 2022.

Dorothy Irene Height

BORN: MARCH 24, 1912, RICHMOND, VA | DIED: APRIL 20, 2010, WASHINGTON, DC

Women know how to get things done.

Dorothy Irene Height was a lifelong activist and leader in the civil rights and women's movements and served as the president of the National Council of Negro Women (NCNW) and an executive in the YWCA. Throughout her life, Dorothy followed her mother's motto, "lifting as we climb." At a very early age, Dorothy became a "joiner," participating in lots of church and school activities including music and sports. She competed in local and national oratory contests, consistently aiming for excellence. Dorothy recalled, "By the time I was twenty-five, I had already shaped my life's work" as a champion of social justice.

During her college years, Dorothy formed important friendships through the Harlem Youth Council. In 1937, Dorothy was on staff at the YWCA when she helped host a meeting of the NCNW. Her encounter with the influential Mary McLeod Bethune and Eleanor Roosevelt was life-changing. Mary was so impressed with Dorothy that she invited her to join the NCNW, and the three women collaborated on projects for almost twenty years.

Dorothy's activism was also fueled by influential meetings with Dr. Benjamin Mays, who introduced her to then-fifteen-year-old student Martin Luther King Jr. Dorothy later used her considerable organizational skills to help plan the 1963 March on Washington, along with the "Big Six" leaders: Martin Luther King Jr., James Farmer, John Lewis, A. Philip Randolph, Roy Wilkins, and Whitney Young. She was the only woman seated on the platform, but she was not invited to speak. Dorothy became an activist for women's rights and organized interracial "Wednesdays in Mississippi," a program that brought Northern and Southern women together to assist student activists operating Freedom Schools, which taught civics and political activism in addition to academic subjects, and encouraged further cooperation.

Dorothy's many awards included the 1994 Presidential Medal of Freedom, the 2004 Congressional Gold Medal, and many honorary doctoral degrees. President Barack Obama dubbed her "the godmother of the civil rights movement."

Misty Copeland

BORN: SEPTEMBER 10, 1982, KANSAS CITY, MO

**I'm 5'2", I started when I was thirteen,
I'm Black, but I've made it happen.
I'm very lucky to be where I am. . . . It's possible.**

Misty Copeland is an award-winning American dancer who in 2015 became the first African American to be named principal ballerina for the prestigious American Ballet Theatre (ABT). A graceful, athletic dance prodigy, Misty began formally studying ballet at the relatively late age of thirteen, when she took lessons at a local Boys & Girls Club in her hometown. In the four years that followed, Misty's rise in the dance world was meteoric.

Misty's parents, Douglas Copeland and Sylvia DelaCerna, divorced when she was a toddler. As a single parent, her mother struggled to provide for Misty and her five siblings. But Sylvia always encouraged her daughter's love of dance, especially when coach Elizabeth Cantine spotted Misty's natural grace and raw talent as she performed on her school's drill team. As Misty's training intensified, she lived apart from her mother for three years, staying with her guardian and manager, Cynthia Bradley.

At fifteen years old, Misty won first place at the Los Angeles Music Center Spotlight Awards; she was later recognized by the *Los Angeles Times* as the best young dancer in the Los Angeles area. Shortly after, she moved to New York City and became a member of ABT at age seventeen. As a soloist, Misty won great acclaim for her starring performance in ABT's production of Igor Stravinsky's *Firebird*.

Major surgery in 2012 to address fractures in her tibia threatened to end Misty's dance career, but with discipline, rigor, and renewed care for her body, Misty returned stronger and more confident than ever, performing starring roles with ABT, including becoming the first African American woman in a professional company to perform the role of Odette/Odile in *Swan Lake* in 2014, dancing with Prince, acting on Broadway, appearing with cellist Yo-Yo Ma, interviewing alongside President Obama, and writing several books. PBS also produced the film *A Ballerina's Tale,* documenting Misty's life and rise to prominence. The "unlikely ballerina" continues to perform with ABT.

Angela Davis

BORN: JANUARY 26, 1944, BIRMINGHAM, AL

I am no longer accepting the things I cannot change.
I am changing the things I cannot accept.

Angela became one of the prominent faces of the African American struggle for freedom and justice. She was greatly influenced by events in her childhood home of Birmingham, Alabama. When she was four, her family moved into a formerly white neighborhood. The following spring, white supremacists bombed the home of their Black neighbor. Bombings became such a constant that her neighborhood was called Dynamite Hill. Years later, the deaths of four girls in the 1963 bombing of the Sixteenth Street Baptist Church made Angela even more committed to the African American civil rights movement.

An excellent student, Angela received a scholarship to Brandeis University and studied abroad in France and Germany. While a graduate student in California, she became active with groups such as the Black Panthers and the Student Nonviolent Coordinating Committee (SNCC). In 1968, she joined a local affiliate of the Communist Party. The next year, California governor Ronald Reagan tried to have her barred from teaching at any university in the state because of her political views. He was not successful, and Angela continued teaching and working on issues such as prison reform.

By 1970, Angela, now an assistant professor at UCLA, was placed on the FBI's most wanted list. She was propelled into the national spotlight after a police shootout in the Marin County courthouse, where four individuals, including a judge, were killed. A warrant was issued for Angela's arrest because the guns used in the shootout were registered to her. The young activist fled.

Angela was eventually captured, and a Free Angela Davis movement supported by African American college students and celebrities sprang up. After sixteen months in prison, she was acquitted in 1972.

Angela resumed teaching at the university level, eventually becoming Distinguished Professor Emerita at UC Santa Cruz. Through her activism, lectures, and scholarship, Angela has been deeply involved in the struggle for social justice and economic, racial, and gender equality.

Ella Fitzgerald

BORN: APRIL 25, 1917, NEWPORT NEWS, VA

DIED: JUNE 15, 1996, BEVERLY HILLS, CA

Just don't give up trying to do what you really want to do. Where there is love and inspiration, I don't think you can go wrong.

The year was 1934. A nervous performer competed in one of the first amateur nights at the famous Apollo Theater. Despite being originally slated to go on as a dancer, at the last minute the young woman changed her mind and sang "Judy" by Hoagy Carmichael. She was Ella Fitzgerald, and she won. Benny Carter, a member of the Apollo house band, was so impressed, he encouraged Ella to keep singing. When she won a chance to perform with Tiny Bradshaw's band, the popular bandleader Chick Webb offered her a tryout. Ella was such a success that Webb hired her to sing with his band. Thus began the career of one of the most honored singers in the history of jazz and popular music.

Ella's teen years were difficult. She had lost her mother, and she frequently skipped school. After being arrested, she was sent to a reform school. Ella ran away from the terrible living conditions there but found herself broke and alone. But as a youngster, Ella had enjoyed dancing and imitating singers she heard on records. Eventually, she would find her stride as an entertainer.

During a career that spanned half a century, Ella recorded more than 200 albums that sold over forty million copies and won thirteen Grammy Awards. She was the first African American to win Grammys, for both the Duke Ellington *and* the Irving Berlin songbooks in 1958. Comfortable singing ballads, moody melodies, and the lightning-fast scat riffs that were her specialty, Ella was one of the most familiar voices in both jazz and pop music. When music lovers heard Ella, they knew they were listening to the First Lady of Song.

Fannie Lou Hamer

BORN: OCTOBER 6, 1917, RULEVILLE, MS

DIED: MARCH 14, 1977, MOUND BAYOU, MS

I am sick and tired of being sick and tired.

Fannie Lou Hamer sat at a table to testify before the Credentials Committee at the 1964 National Democratic Convention. She spoke plainly, powerfully, and passionately, detailing her efforts and those of the Mississippi Freedom Democratic Party (MFDP) to register to vote as first-class citizens of the United States. In her state, Blacks were not represented by the Democratic Party. If the MFDP was not recognized and seated, Fannie stated in front of the television cameras, "I question America."

Fannie was an activist, an orator, a community organizer, and a courageous leader of the civil rights movement during the 1960s and 1970s. Born and raised on Mississippi cotton plantations where she and members of her family were sharecroppers, Fannie didn't realize she had the right to vote until she was forty-four years old.

Fannie was a fearless freedom fighter during a time when less than two percent of the Black population in Mississippi was registered to vote and such activism was dangerous. Fannie was evicted from her home in Ruleville for trying to register, she was brutally beaten for organizing, and her family and friends were shot at to deter her activism.

Despite these efforts to silence her, Fannie continued to raise her voice, even teaching citizenship classes to help educate her neighbors about their voting rights. She sang African American spirituals as a part of her speeches to inspire and encourage others to continue challenging the system of white supremacy. She cofounded the MFDP and confronted the all-white delegation. Although not seated in 1964, by the 1968 Democratic Convention, the MFDP became the official delegation of the state. That year Fannie also organized a local Freedom Farm and pig bank, mobilizing her community to raise food to feed themselves. In 1971, she ran for Congress. Nationally and locally, Fannie was tireless in her efforts to organize women and poor people.

Although she had a powerful, charismatic presence, poor health from childhood polio, diabetes, cancer, and complications from brutal beatings contributed to her death at the age of fifty-nine, in 1977.

Elizabeth Catlett

BORN: APRIL 15, 1915, WASHINGTON, DC

DIED: APRIL 2, 2012, CUERNAVACA, MEXICO

**I have always wanted my art to service
my people—to reflect us, to relate to us,
to stimulate us, to make us aware of our potential.**

Elizabeth Catlett was an internationally known printmaker and sculptor whose art was always fiercely socially conscious. Her signature pieces focused on African Americans, women, and the lives of working-class people. Part of her goal as an activist "womanist" artist was to make political statements and to make her work accessible to everyone. In bold strokes, she carved a series of fifteen linocuts with titles like *Survivor, Sharecropper,* and *Negro Mother* in an epic commemoration of the historic oppression, resistance, and survival of African American women. Linocuts based on her sculpture *Mother and Child,* which won first prize at the 1940 American Negro Exposition in Chicago, had a major effect on the art world. Elizabeth became one of the most prominent African American artists of the twentieth century.

Elizabeth earned a scholarship to the Carnegie Institute of Technology but was denied admission when school administrators learned that she was Black. Undaunted, she enrolled at Howard University, where her teachers included painter Lois Mailou Jones, art historian James Porter, and philosopher Alain Locke. Later, she studied with Grant Wood at the University of Iowa, where she was the first African American to earn a Master of Fine Arts degree.

After teaching at several African American institutions, in 1946 she was awarded a Rosenwald fellowship. She traveled to Mexico City, where she was invited to work at the Taller de Gráfica Popular, an artists' collective dedicated to graphic arts that promoted leftist political causes, social issues, and education. Elizabeth forged friendships with Diego Rivera, Miguel Covarrubias, David Siqueiros, Frida Kahlo, and other socially conscious artists from the African diaspora. Elizabeth became the first female professor of sculpture in the National Fine Arts School at the Universidad Nacional Autónoma de México, and later served as chair of the sculpture department.

Elizabeth's work can be found in major collections at the Museum of Modern Art, the Metropolitan Museum of Art, and the Library of Congress. Art historian Melanie Herzog called her "the foremost African American woman artist of her generation."

Serena Williams

BORN: SEPTEMBER 26, 1981, SAGINAW, MI

I really think a champion is defined not by their wins but by how they can recover when they fall.

During a stellar career, Serena Williams is credited, along with her sister Venus, for ushering in a new arena of boldness, strength, and athleticism in women's tennis. Serena is an award-winning African American tennis player who has won title after title since joining the ranks of women's professional tennis as a teenager in 1995. Strong, independent, and talented, Serena has been hailed as one of the best female tennis players in the Open Era. First ranked number one in the world for female tennis players at the age of twenty, she has won twenty-three Grand Slam singles titles, fourteen Grand Slam doubles titles (all with her sister Venus), four Olympic gold medals, and numerous additional championships. She was the only woman on the 2017 *Forbes* list of the 100 highest-paid athletes.

Serena began playing tennis at the age of three on urban tennis courts in Compton, California. Under her father Richard's tutelage, Serena developed an explosive serve and a signature two-handed backhand. Always highly competitive, Serena continued to excel on the court in spite of criticism and derogatory racial comments aimed at her clothing, hair, and unorthodox, powerful style of play.

At age nine, Serena moved with her family to West Palm Beach, Florida, where she and Venus attended Rick Macci's tennis academy. In 1995, when Serena was in the ninth grade, her father took over her coaching after disagreements with Macci.

During her tennis career, Serena experienced multiple injuries; a life-threatening pulmonary embolism; the birth of her first child, Alexis Olympia Ohanian Jr.; and multiple comebacks. She has succeeded both on and off the court, with celebrity status, product endorsements, an apparel line, fashion and media appearances, philanthropy, and serving as a role model for young female athletes and an ambassador of tennis. The story of the Williams family also served as inspiration for the Oscar-winning film *King Richard*. Some have heralded Serena as the GOAT, or the Greatest of All Time.

Phillis Wheatley

BORN: C. 1753, SENEGAL-GAMBIA, WEST AFRICA

DIED: DECEMBER 5, 1784, BOSTON, MA

**In every human Breast, God has implanted
a Principle, which we call Love of Freedom;
it is impatient of Oppression, and pants for Deliverance.**

Phillis Wheatley was the first Black female poet to be published in the United States and also the first person of African heritage to make a living as a writer here. Her book, *Poems on Various Subjects, Religious and Moral,* was published in 1773, and her individual poems were widely read during the colonial era. Phillis's fame as a poet was also heralded in England, and she visited there in 1771.

Phillis was born around 1753 and was kidnapped from her home in the Senegal-Gambia region of West Africa. Transported to America in 1761, she was purchased by a wealthy Boston tailor, John Wheatley. Phillis quickly mastered speaking English, and with the help of the Wheatleys' two children, she also learned to read and write. Phillis read the Bible and classic works by Homer, Virgil, John Milton, and Alexander Pope. By 1770, she had written and published her poem "An Elegiac Poem, on the Death of that Celebrated Divine, and Eminent Servant of Jesus Christ, the Reverend and Learned George Whitefield." Phillis received international acclaim in the abolitionist and literary circles of New England and Philadelphia.

Phillis was particularly fond of the couplet as a poetic form, and infused Biblical symbolism and references to the patriotism of the early revolutionists. Race is a theme in her first collection of thirty-nine poems, among them "On Being Brought from Africa to America," which is often anthologized in poetry collections.

During her lifetime, Phillis's talent was heralded by President George Washington and others with whom she corresponded. Massachusetts governor Thomas Hutchinson and signers of the Declaration of Independence Benjamin Rush and John Hancock attested to her intelligence and her skill as a poet.

Phillis was freed from slavery after her master's death in 1774. In 1778, she married a free Black man, John Peters, and continued to write, despite her husband's economic insecurity and her own failing health. She completed a second volume of poems, but she was not able to raise enough money to have them published.

Rosa Parks

BORN: FEBRUARY 4, 1913, TUSKEGEE, AL | **DIED:** OCTOBER 24, 2005, DETROIT, MI

The only tired I was, was tired of giving in.

Rosa Parks was a feisty child who questioned Jim Crow laws and the injustices she saw around her. She carried that fighting spirit with her into adulthood, especially on one Montgomery, Alabama, day in 1955. On December 1, Rosa resisted bus driver James F. Blake's order to move from the white section to the colored section on the Cleveland Avenue bus. Because she didn't give up her seat, she was charged with violating Chapter 6, Section 11 of the city code and was arrested. By December 5, members of the African American community formed the Montgomery Improvement Association (MIA) and elected Rev. Dr. Martin Luther King Jr. as its leader. The MIA then organized the Montgomery bus boycott, which lasted more than a year.

As a result of her activism, Rosa and her husband, Raymond, lost their jobs, faced violence and death threats, and were forced to relocate to Detroit, Michigan. Rosa, however, remained committed to the struggle for civil rights throughout her life and was later revered as the Mother of the Movement. Her simple act of protest against unjust segregation laws triggered a mass call to action throughout the United States in the decades-long struggle for civil rights.

Rosa was born in Tuskegee, Alabama, to Leona Edwards McCauley, a teacher, and James McCauley, a carpenter. Rosa had to leave high school to care for her ailing grandmother, but later obtained her high school diploma. She worked alongside her activist husband during the 1930s in his support of the Scottsboro Boys, teens who were falsely accused of committing a violent crime against two white women. Rosa became secretary of the local NAACP in 1943, supported voter registration campaigns and wrongfully accused Black men, and fought for the desegregation of schools and public places. She attended the Highlander Folk School in Tennessee, a center for training activists for workers' rights and racial equality.

In Detroit, Rosa worked in the office of Representative John Conyers from 1965 until her retirement in 1987. She also remained active in civil rights, the Black Power movement, and support of political prisoners in the United States. Her life was filled with accolades, including the NAACP Spingarn Medal, the Presidential Medal of Freedom, the Congressional Gold Medal, and dozens of honorary degrees. After her death at age ninety-two, her body lay in honor in the US Capitol, the first woman so recognized.

Leontyne Price

BORN: FEBRUARY 10, 1927, LAUREL, MS

**The color of my skin or the kink of my hair
or the spread of my mouth has nothing
to do with what you are listening to.**

Leontyne Price is a lyric soprano who was the first leading African American prima donna to perform with the New York Metropolitan Opera. When she performed *Il Trovatore* on January 27, 1961, she received an ovation that lasted forty-two minutes, one of the longest in Met history. Leontyne's voice has been described as "luscious, warm, buttery, rich, vibrant, voluminous, and soaring." During her tenure at the Met, she received the highest of praise while singing leading roles in *Madama Butterfly, Tosca, Aida, Falstaff, Don Giovanni, Porgy and Bess,* and *Antony and Cleopatra,* among many others. Critic Harold C. Schonberg wrote in a *New York Times* review, "Voice is what counts, and voice is what Miss Price has."

Mary Violet Leontyne Price's parents recognized their daughter's extraordinary musical gifts early on. At age three, they bought her a toy piano. Leontyne began piano lessons in her Mississippi hometown, and by the time she was in kindergarten, her parents traded in the family phonograph as the down payment for an upright piano. Leontyne was nine years old when she heard Marian Anderson sing in a concert in Jackson, Mississippi, and decided on a career as an opera singer.

From her humble beginnings, Leontyne went on to study music education at Wilberforce College in Ohio and voice at the Juilliard School. She made her recital debut at New York's Town Hall in November 1954, and she was the first African American to sing a leading opera role on national television. Leontyne performed nationally and internationally, and in May 1960, she made her first appearance in a leading role at La Scala in Milan, Italy. Leontyne performed highly successful concerts and recitals throughout the 1970s.

She retired from opera in 1985 but continued to perform until 1997. Her concert programs usually combined Handel arias, German Lieder, and French and American art songs, and ended with spirituals.

Among her many accomplishments, Leontyne won nineteen Grammys, the NAACP Spingarn Medal, a Kennedy Center Honor, and the National Medal of Arts.

Harriet Tubman

BORN: C. 1820, DORCHESTER COUNTY, MD | DIED: MARCH 10, 1913, AUBURN, NY

(T)here was one of two things I had a right to, liberty or death; if I could not have one, I would have the other.

Harriet Tubman was a conductor on the Underground Railroad and was known as the Moses of Her People. She developed visionary leadership skills while enslaved with her parents on a Maryland plantation. Originally named Araminta "Minty" Ross, she took the name Harriet (in honor of her mother) Tubman when she married. She freed herself on September 17, 1849, when she was roughly twenty-nine years old.

Harriet's journey to freedom was arduous. In spite of her small size and sickly nature, she was hired out to work for other households at age five. Later she had to set traps for muskrats, do farmwork, and haul logs along a river. Following a severe head injury, Araminta began to have seizures, which caused premonitions that God was speaking to her. These visions strengthened her resolve to be free. After escaping and traveling ninety miles to Pennsylvania via the Underground Railroad, Harriet worked to free her family and friends. She made more than a dozen trips back to Maryland during an eleven-year period and led more than three hundred people out of bondage to Pennsylvania and Canada.

Harriet worked with abolitionists John Brown, Frederick Douglass, William Still, and others prior to the Civil War. During the war, she served as a spy, an army nurse, and a scout, and she was the first woman to lead an armed expedition in a raid, along the Combahee River in South Carolina. There she helped to free more than 750 enslaved people.

After the Civil War, she retired to Auburn, New York, where she established a home with the local AME church for her aged parents and for indigents who needed care. She worked with Elizabeth Cady Stanton and Susan B. Anthony on behalf of women's suffrage and equal rights. After thirty years of petitioning the government, she finally received an army pension starting at eight dollars per month, but she struggled financially for much of her life. When Harriet died at age ninety-three, she was buried with semi-military honors at Fort Hill Cemetery in Auburn. Harriet will be the first African American whose likeness appears on US currency.

Ruby Dee

BORN: OCTOBER 27, 1922, CLEVELAND, OH
DIED: JUNE 11, 2014, NEW ROCHELLE, NY

The greatest gift is not being afraid to question.

Ruby Dee wanted to be an actress, but the chances for success did not look promising. There were very few professional opportunities for African Americans during the 1940s. Ruby joined the American Negro Theatre (ANT), a fledging group that included Sidney Poitier, Harry Belafonte, and Ossie Davis. They rehearsed in the basement of the Harlem branch of the New York Public Library, and she was in that group's first production, *On Striver's Row.* From that historic beginning, Ruby's career would span seven decades.

Ruby appeared in the movies *Edge of the City* with Sidney Poitier and *A Raisin in the Sun,* based on the play by Lorraine Hansberry. Her television movie credits include *I Know Why the Caged Bird Sings,* based on Maya Angelou's famous memoir, and *Roots: The Next Generations.* She was also the first Black actress to appear on the popular TV soap opera *Peyton Place,* and she was featured in Spike Lee's films *Do the Right Thing* and *Jungle Fever.* Onstage, Ruby became the first Black actress to play major roles at the American Shakespeare Festival.

Longtime civil rights activists, Ruby and her husband, Ossie Davis, were members of the National Association for the Advancement of Colored People (NAACP), the Student Nonviolent Coordinating Committee (SNCC), the Southern Christian Leadership Conference (SCLC), and the Congress of Racial Equality (CORE). They were close friends of Dr. Martin Luther King Jr. and Malcolm X and served as masters of ceremony at the 1963 March on Washington. In 1995, the couple, affectionately known as "the first couple of Black theater," was awarded the National Medal of Arts. In 2008, Ruby received the NAACP's prestigious Spingarn Medal for her acting, writing, and social justice work. She left an enduring legacy on stage, screen, television, and radio.

Zora Neale Hurston

BORN: JANUARY 7, 1891, NOTASULGA, AL
DIED: JANUARY 28, 1960, FORT PIERCE, FL

Research is formalized curiosity.
It is poking and prying with a purpose.

Zora Neale Hurston's mother, a former schoolteacher, encouraged Zora to "jump at the sun" and explore the creative talents she expressed as a child, despite her father's efforts to tame her rebellious spirit. Zora followed her mother's advice and engaged in numerous adventures on her path to literary success. Zora was a somewhat controversial personality because she used African American dialect in some of her writing. She could be outspoken, and sometimes she expressed unpopular political views.

Zora was a novelist, folklorist, anthropologist, and influential member of the community of artists and writers of the Harlem Renaissance. She was a contemporary of and onetime collaborator with Langston Hughes. She wrote four novels, several musicals, and more than fifty short stories. As an anthropologist, Zora conducted documentary research on cultural rituals in Jamaica and Haiti. Her most famous work is the novel *Their Eyes Were Watching God*.

Born in her grandparents' hometown of Notasulga, Alabama, Zora later moved with her parents, Lucy Ann and John Hurston, and siblings to Eatonville, Florida, an independent, self-governing Black town where her father was elected mayor in 1897. Zora used many of the town personalities as models for characters in her stories.

During Franklin Roosevelt's administration, Zora worked for the WPA in New York City and in the South as a freelance newspaper reporter and a substitute teacher, and in a variety of odd jobs to support her career as a writer. Although she traveled extensively, utilizing her rich academic background and literary skills, Zora died in relative obscurity, without financial stability. She was buried in an unmarked grave. Alice Walker is credited with reviving interest in Zora's career in her 1979 *Ms.* magazine article, "In Search of Zora Neale Hurston." Zora's work is now celebrated annually at literature festivals in Eatonville and throughout the United States.

Mae C. Jemison

BORN: OCTOBER 17, 1956, DECATUR, AL

Don't let anyone rob you of your imagination, your creativity, or your curiosity.

From the time she was a little girl, Mae C. Jemison was fascinated by the world around her. Her insatiable curiosity led her to the study of nature, science, dance, African American history, astronomy, languages, engineering, medicine, technology, and eventually space. Mae was the first African American woman to participate in NASA's space program. Starting September 12, 1992, as a Mission Specialist, she orbited the earth 126 times in the space shuttle *Endeavour*. She carried with her an Alvin Ailey dance poster, several art objects from West Africa, and a photo of airplane pilot Bessie Coleman. Mae felt that science and dance were "expressions of the boundless creativity that people have to share with one another."

Growing up, Mae was captivated with science, the arts, and dance, which she began studying when she was eleven. She was an excellent student, entering college at the age of sixteen and graduating from Stanford University in 1977 with a degree in chemical engineering. During this time, she also continued her pursuit of dance and African and Afro-American studies. After graduating from Cornell Medical College in 1981, Mae served as a Peace Corps medical officer in Liberia and Sierra Leone from 1983 to 1985.

Mae's childhood dreams of "going into space" were realized when she was accepted into NASA's training program in 1986. Five years later, during the shuttle mission, she conducted experiments in life sciences and material sciences and was co-investigator in the bone cell research experiment.

Mae resigned from NASA in 1993 to continue pursuing her interests in medicine, technology, and social sciences. As an author, public speaker, and college professor, Mae is an advocate for the study of sciences and technology, especially for minorities. Her company, the Jemison Group, develops and markets advanced technologies for daily life. She has inspired generations of young people by establishing an international science camp for high school students and other innovative programs in the United States and developing countries.

Susie King Taylor

BORN: AUGUST 6, 1848, LIBERTY COUNTY, GA

DIED: OCTOBER 6, 1912, BOSTON, MA

I gave my services willingly . . . without receiving a dollar.

Susie King Taylor became the first Black army nurse during the Civil War. She openly taught former slaves in a school in Georgia when it was against the law to teach Black people to read, and she published *Reminiscences of My Life in Camp with the 33rd United States Colored Troops, Late 1st S.C. Volunteers,* about her experience during the Civil War.

Susie was enslaved, but her grandmother, Dolly Reed, was a free woman who lived in Savannah, Georgia, nearly thirty-five miles from the Grest plantation where Susie was born. When Susie was seven years old, she and her brother were sent to live with their grandmother, and they learned to read and write at a secret school for Blacks run by her grandmother's neighbor, Mrs. Woodhouse.

During the Civil War, Susie was sent back to the Grest plantation. Soon after, she and some other members of her family were taken by boat by Union forces to St. Simon's Island. When Union officers learned that she could read, they asked Susie to teach formerly enslaved Black soldiers to read and write. Susie taught children during the day and adults at night. She married Edward King and served as a nurse and laundress for her husband's regiment. She traveled with the regiment for three years and later worked alongside nurse Clara Barton, who founded the Red Cross.

Years later, Susie wrote in her memoir:

> I was very happy to know my efforts were successful in camp, and also felt grateful for the appreciation of my services. I gave my services willingly for four years and three months without receiving a dollar. I was glad, however, to be allowed to go with the regiment, to care for the sick and afflicted comrades.

At the end of the war, Susie and Edward moved back to Savannah, and in 1866, she established a private school for freed children. She taught until the 1870s, when her students were allowed to attend public school for free. Susie was dedicated to teaching and to service, but after the birth of her child and the death of her husband, she took a job as a domestic with a wealthy white family and traveled with them to Boston. Her love of nursing and education continued, however, and she became president of the Woman's Relief Corps, a national association for veterans of the Civil War.

Loretta Lynch

BORN: MAY 21, 1959, GREENSBORO, NC

**I will wake up every morning with the protection
of the American people my first thought.**

Loretta Lynch became the first African American woman to serve as US attorney general when she succeeded Eric Holder, who was also appointed by President Barack Obama.

Loretta was exposed to the causes of social justice from an early age. She literally rode on her father Lorenzo's shoulders during the early years of student lunch-counter sit-in demonstrations and boycotts of the 1960s. She also attended many court proceedings in Durham, North Carolina, with him. Loretta listened to her grandfather's stories about helping other sharecroppers in the South escape to the North to avoid Jim Crow laws. She was inspired by her mother, Lorine, a school librarian, and her Baptist minister father, who offered the basement of his church to students who were organizing sit-ins to protest segregation.

As a student, Loretta was very focused. She expected and respected excellence, professionalism, and attention to detail. After receiving her Harvard law degree, Loretta worked briefly in private practice. She went on to become a federal prosecutor in 1990, then an assistant prosecutor in the US Attorney's Office, eventually rising to US Attorney for the Eastern District of New York. There she forged an impressive career as a prosecutor of violent crimes, civil rights violations, and in 1997, the high-profile case of Abner Louima, a Haitian immigrant who was brutally assaulted by uniformed New York City police officers. Under her leadership, the office successfully prosecuted numerous cases involving corrupt public officials, cybercriminals, and terrorists. Loretta also served on the board of the Federal Reserve Bank from 2003 until 2005.

On November 8, 2014, President Barack Obama nominated Loretta Lynch as US attorney general. After lengthy Senate delays, she was confirmed by the Senate Judiciary Committee on February 26, 2015, and sworn in on April 27. She stopped serving as attorney general in January 2017 and is now working in the private sector as a litigation partner at Paul, Weiss, Rifkind, Wharton & Garrison, a high-profile New York law firm.

Maya Angelou

BORN: APRIL 4, 1928, ST. LOUIS, MO | DIED: MAY 28, 2014, WINSTON-SALEM, NC

While one may encounter many defeats, one must not be defeated.

Her birth name was Marguerite Johnson, but her brother called her Maya. A sexual trauma at the age of seven rendered her mute, but after five years of refusing to speak, Maya eventually reclaimed her voice with the help of a caring teacher who encouraged her to read and write poetry.

While living in Oakland, California, Maya began taking modern dance classes. There she met Alvin Ailey, and the two formed a dance team called Al and Rita. Thus began Maya's journey of personal artistic discovery through poetry, dance, acting, filmmaking, journalism, music, and lifelong activism for social justice. She cultivated relationships with many important friends and mentors, including writers James Baldwin, John Oliver Killens, and Rosa Guy, actors Harry Belafonte and Abby Lincoln, activist Malcolm X, civil rights leader Dr. Martin Luther King Jr., for whom she served as a Southern Christian Leadership Conference (SCLC) coordinator during the 1960s, and entrepreneur Oprah Winfrey.

A multitalented writer and performer, Maya commanded attention with her statuesque, six-foot-tall figure; her deep, dramatic voice; and her pithy, memorable memoirs. She was an award-winning and internationally recognized writer of seven memoirs, children's books, screenplays, articles, and essays. Her first memoir, *I Know Why the Caged Bird Sings,* published in 1969, was a runaway bestseller. Maya was also an accomplished actress and dancer and was the first Black female movie director in Hollywood.

In 1993, Maya recited her poem "On the Pulse of Morning" at the inauguration of President Bill Clinton. She was honored with the Presidential Medal of Freedom by President Barack Obama in 2011. Two years later, the National Book Award Foundation gave her the Literarian Award. She also received over fifty honorary doctoral degrees.

Beyoncé Knowles-Carter

BORN: SEPTEMBER 4, 1981, HOUSTON, TX

**I have learned that it is no one else's job
to take care of me but me.**

Bathed in golden lights, surrounded by dazzling sound, and energized with incredible beats and choreography, Beyoncé Knowles-Carter dominates stage and video performances with her compelling lyrics, velvet vocals, provocative dance moves, and commanding stage presence. Beyoncé is a multitalented American R&B and pop singer, songwriter, entertainer, dancer, actress, and music producer. She is also one of the bestselling music artists in history, with twenty-eight Grammy Awards (and seventy-nine nominations) and counting. Famous for "slaying" her audiences, Beyoncé is the most nominated woman in the history of the music awards.

Beyoncé was born and raised in Houston by her parents, Celestine "Tina" Knowles, a hairdresser, designer, and salon owner, and Mathew Knowles, a sales manager. She took dance lessons at an early age and by eight was performing on the talent-show circuit in Houston. She became part of the all-girl band Girl's Tyme, which later morphed into Destiny's Child and sold more than 60 million albums between 1996 and 2005.

As a solo artist, Beyoncé has also been known as Sasha Fierce and Queen Bey. She has pursued acting opportunities in film and television movies, such as *The Pink Panther, Dreamgirls,* and *Austin Powers in Goldmember.*

Her performances on MTV, the BET Awards, and the Super Bowl XLVII and Super Bowl 50 halftime shows and her amazing world tours have solidified Beyoncé's position as an international pop icon. *Dangerously in Love,* Beyoncé's first solo album, featured rapper-producer and future husband Jay-Z in "Crazy in Love," her first number-one single as a solo artist.

Themes of female empowerment infuse her songwriting, performances, and social justice activities. Among her inspirations are musicians Michael Jackson, Diana Ross, Whitney Houston, Mariah Carey, and Etta James, and First Lady Michelle Obama.

The ongoing successes of *Lemonade,* 2016's bestselling album worldwide, and *Everything Is Love,* Beyoncé's 2018 release with Jay-Z, show how she continues to shape and influence the entertainment industry and popular culture at large.

Simone Biles

BORN: MARCH 14, 1997, COLUMBUS, OH

I'd rather regret the risks that didn't work out than the chances I didn't take at all.

Simone Biles stepped onto the floor mat and started running. In seconds, this petite, powerful athlete was tumbling in the air, defying gravity. Sticking the dismount, Simone flashed a brilliant smile and waved to the adoring crowd.

Simone is a seven-time Olympic medalist gymnast whose phenomenal artistry and athleticism have won her accolades across the globe. At the 2016 Summer Olympics, Simone won four gold medals with stunning performances in the team, all-around, vault, and floor competitions, and a bronze medal for beam. She competed at the 2020 Summer Olympics and won silver in the team competition and bronze on the balance beam. With a total of thirty-two medals at the Olympics and world championships, Simone is the most decorated gymnast in the history of the sport.

Her remarkable gymnastics journey began on a field trip to a gym in Houston. Only two years earlier, she had been in and out of foster care in Columbus, Ohio, because her birth mother, who struggled with addiction, was unable to care for her and her siblings. Simone and her sister were adopted by her grandfather Ron and his wife, Nellie Biles, who signed her up for gymnastics classes near their Texas home. Simone's talent and fearlessness were immediately apparent.

She began to seriously train at age eight, and in 2011 started competing locally, nationally, and internationally. To increase her rigorous physical training from twenty to thirty-two hours a week, Simone was homeschooled during her high school years.

From 2012 through 2021, Simone intensified her skills—even developing four now named in her honor—and participated in the largest national and international competitions, including the American Cup, world championships, Olympic trials, and finally the Olympic Games. At the Rio Games, Team USA chose Simone to carry the flag in the closing ceremonies. Simone took a hiatus from competition in 2017. She had a stint on ABC's *Dancing with the Stars* and collaborated on the television film *The Simone Biles Story: Courage to Soar.* After the 2020 Olympic Games, Simone became an outspoken advocate for mental health awareness.

Ava DuVernay

BORN: AUGUST 24, 1972, LONG BEACH, CA

Figure out what you need to do
to be the heroine of your own story.

A *Wrinkle in Time, Selma, 13th, I Will Follow, Middle of Nowhere, This Is the Life:* Ava directed all of them. As a child, she planned and directed her younger sisters and their Barbie dolls by scripting imaginary story lines and adventures for them. Today Ava is an award-winning director who has achieved a number of firsts in cinema for Black women. She won a best director prize at Sundance, her film was nominated for an Oscar, and she was the first to direct a $100 million film, *A Wrinkle in Time.*

"I didn't start out thinking that I could ever make films," Ava says. "I started out being a film lover, loving films, and wanting to have a job that put me close to them and close to the filmmakers and close to film sets." After graduating from UCLA, Ava worked as a publicist before forming her own agency in 1999. The DuVernay Agency (later known as DVA Media + Marketing) provided award-winning PR services for over 100 high-profile film and television projects.

Ava's first film, *This Is the Life,* documented the hip-hop scene at a café where she had performed. In *Selma,* Ava chronicled Dr. Martin Luther King Jr.'s leadership and struggle for voting rights. The Oscar-nominated documentary *13th* explores American race relations and the contemporary justice system. Her TV miniseries *When They See Us,* about five New York City teens falsely accused and wrongfully convicted of a brutal attack in Central Park, is a searing indictment of racism, media bias, and the failures of the legal system. Ava is committed to using the power of the screen to expose truth and to effect change.

While forging her own career path, Ava has been an activist and an advocate for diversity in the motion picture industry. As a writer, producer, and director for the popular television series *Queen Sugar, Naomi,* and *Wings of Fire,* Ava has employed female scriptwriters, production crews, and actors. Array, her film-distribution company, utilizes the skills and services of people of color. Ava recognizes that her influence is a privilege. She is not satisfied with being the "first" or the only Black woman in the room. She wants to create and extend creative opportunities for others.

Judith Jamison

BORN: MAY 10, 1943, PHILADELPHIA, PA

If you look at a dancer in silence, his or her body will be the music. . . .

In her signature performance of Alvin Ailey's "Cry," Judith Jamison moved with fluid and electrifying elegance—transforming a long white piece of cloth into a child, a washrag, an ironing board, and a shawl, from the embodiment of an enslaved woman carrying "the weight of the world" to exemplifying a liberated woman's ecstasy and grace. The three-part, fifteen-minute performance was created especially for Judith by choreographer Alvin Ailey as an expression to honor all Black mothers. Through Judith's body—her long arms and legs and regal carriage—dance became an extraordinary "medium for honoring the past, celebrating the present and fearlessly reaching into the future."

The daughter of blue-collar Black parents, Judith started taking ballet classes when she was six years old, and she was embraced by her family and church community. She learned about commitment to excellence and helping others, strengths she has relied on throughout her stellar career.

Judith trained at the Philadelphia Dance Academy until Agnes de Mille of the American Ballet Theater invited her to perform her newest work, *The Four Marys*. At the close of the show in 1964, Judith was left without a job, but soon an audition and a series of connections led her to accept a position at Alvin Ailey in 1965. As a member of the Alvin Ailey American Dance Theater (AAADT), Judith helped to redefine the world's perception of American dance with her commanding presence. She performed with the AAADT for over fifteen years before launching a solo career on Broadway in 1980, and a few years later her own company, the Jamison Project. After Alvin's death in 1989, she directed the AAADT for twenty-one years. Judith served as artistic director, teacher, and choreographer and played a major role in raising the funds for the construction of a permanent $54 million, eight-floor building for the company, which opened in 2005.

Judith retired from her position as artistic director in 2011 but continues to influence the creative world as a choreographer and educator. Her many honors include the National Medal of Arts, the Congressional Black Caucus's Phoenix Award, a Kennedy Center Honor for her contribution to American culture through dance, and being named NYC Ambassador of the Arts.

Oprah Winfrey

BORN: JANUARY 29, 1954, KOSCIUSKO, MS

You get in life what you have the courage to ask for.

Very few people are recognized by one name, but Oprah is one of them. She is known worldwide as a glamorous media mogul, successful business owner, television and movie star, billionaire, and philanthropist. Oprah's name is also her brand.

From the time she was a very young child, Oprah Winfrey knew that she had a big voice inside of her that was waiting to be heard. Born to a teenage single mother, Oprah lived in poverty with her maternal grandmother in rural Mississippi, followed by a troubled home life with her mother in Milwaukee, where she was physically and sexually abused by male relatives. Finally, in Nashville, Tennessee, her father provided a stable home life. Oprah became an honor student, was voted her high school's most popular girl, joined the speech team, and won a scholarship to Tennessee State University. After winning a Miss Black Tennessee beauty contest at age seventeen, she got a job broadcasting the news part-time on a local Black radio station. She was so impressive that, at nineteen, Oprah became Nashville's youngest and first Black female television news anchor at WLAC-TV, and was recruited to co-anchor the six o'clock news at WJZ-TV in Baltimore.

In 1986, Oprah moved to Chicago to host a failing half-hour morning talk show, and within a year, *AM Chicago* was a hit. She expanded the program to an hour and renamed it *The Oprah Winfrey Show,* which became one of the most successful television shows for twenty-five years. In 2011, Oprah launched her own cable channel called OWN: Oprah Winfrey Network.

As an actress, Oprah has appeared in the TV miniseries *The Women of Brewster Place* and in such movies as *The Color Purple, Beloved,* and *A Wrinkle in Time.* Her company, Harpo Productions, has developed and produced documentaries, films, and a Broadway musical of *The Color Purple.* Oprah is also the publisher of the popular magazine *O.*

Oprah has used her voice and her wealth to support social justice, the arts, and education, including the Oprah Winfrey Leadership Academy for Girls in South Africa. Her many awards and honors include being named the first recipient of the Bob Hope Humanitarian Award. She was also awarded the Presidential Medal of Freedom by President Barack Obama.

Black Lives Matter:
Patrisse Cullors, Alicia Garza, Ayọ Tometi

We are a generation called to action. —Patrisse Cullors

When Black people get free, everybody gets free. —Alicia Garza

I challenge us all to have the courage of our convictions to fight for a fair, just, and inclusive society. —Ayọ Tometi

Patrisse Cullors (bottom), Alicia Garza (top), and Ayọ Tometi (middle) created a national movement by organizing themselves and others around the hashtag #BlackLivesMatter. It was their response to George Zimmerman's acquittal for the 2012 murder of seventeen-year-old Trayvon Martin. Stunned by the verdict and determined that this gross injustice would not happen again, these gifted women pooled their skills and commitment in a public call to action to combat oppression.

Now global in scope, #BlackLivesMatter affirms Black life in the face of systemic police brutality, mass incarceration, racism, and prejudice of all kinds. This includes supporting Black women, queer and transgender folks, people with disabilities, the Black-undocumented, and those with criminal records. In 2021, Black Lives Matter was nominated for the Nobel Peace Prize.

Patrisse Cullors (born in 1984) is an artist, organizer, educator, and performance artist, active in many causes in the Los Angeles community, including prison abolition. She believes that "curiosity is a foundation for activism."

Alicia Garza (born in 1981) is an activist, writer, and community organizer who directs special projects at the National Domestic Workers Alliance in the San Francisco Bay Area. Alicia wrote three words at the end of a Facebook post: "Black lives matter." She is now the cofounder of the organization of the same name.

Ayọ (formerly Opal) Tometi (born in 1984) is a Nigerian American writer and organizer from New York, who developed the social media strategies of the BLM platform. She is also executive director of Black Alliance for Just Immigration (BAJI), created in response to anti-immigrant sentiment and repressive immigration bills.

The #BlackLivesMatter movement has forced many in America to confront the legacy of racism and inspires those who are concerned about justice and equality.

Learn More About the Women of *Brave. Black. First.*

MARIAN ANDERSON

- Nickname: Baby Contralto
- At the Lincoln Memorial, altered the lyric "Of thee I sing" to "Of thee we sing," later explaining, "We cannot live alone. . . . And the thing that made this moment possible for you and for me has been brought about by many people whom we will never know."
- Autobiography: *My Lord, What a Morning*
- Shopped at Mae's Millinery, a hat boutique owned by Mae Reeves in Philadelphia
- Attended the launch of the American Liberty ship SS *Booker T. Washington* with Mary McLeod Bethune on September 29, 1942, the first of seventeen Liberty ships named in honor of African Americans

Maya Angelou in conversation with Hillary Clinton at Wake Forest University on April 18, 2008.

MAYA ANGELOU

- First Black female streetcar conductor in San Francisco; received a lifetime achievement award in 2014 from the Conference of Minority Transportation Officials for her work
- Proficient in six languages: English, Fante, French, Hebrew, Italian, and Spanish
- Received three Grammy Award nominations for spoken-word albums
- The first Black woman to write a released screenplay (*Georgia, Georgia*) and direct a major motion picture, *Down in the Delta*
- Completed last memoir, *Mom & Me & Mom,* at age eighty-five
- Personal papers and career memorabilia can be found at the Schomburg Center for Research in Black Culture in Harlem, including handwritten notes on yellow legal pads for *I Know Why the Caged Bird Sings.*
- Close friend and mentor to Oprah Winfrey

Marian Anderson singing on the steps of the Lincoln Memorial on April 9, 1939. She sang for twenty-five minutes. The mink coat she wore that cool Easter day is preserved at the Anacostia Community Museum in Washington, DC.

MARY McLEOD BETHUNE

- Nicknames: First Lady of the Struggle, Mama Bethune
- Close friend of Eleanor Roosevelt and advisor to several US presidents, including Calvin Coolidge and Franklin D. Roosevelt

A pastel painting by Winold Reiss in 1925 honoring the legacy of Mary McLeod Bethune. The portrait hangs in the National Portrait Gallery.

- Led voter registration drives for African Americans and women
- The only woman of color present at the founding conference of the United Nations in 1945
- Often walked with a cane, not out of necessity but because it gave her "swank"
- Home in Washington, DC, is a registered National Historic Site and is open to the public

SIMONE BILES

- Has four skills named the Biles in her honor in the Artistic Gymnastics Code of Points
- Has dual citizenship in America and Belize and considers Belize her second home
- An outspoken advocate for children in the foster care system and sexual-abuse survivors
- First female gymnast to win three consecutive world all-around titles
- Named one of *Time*'s Most Influential People in the World in 2017
- In 2014, became the first American female gymnast to win four gold medals at a single world championships
- Won nineteen world championship gold medals, the most by any gymnast in history

BLACK LIVES MATTER

A logo for the Black Lives Matter political and ideological movement.

BLACK LIVES MATTER

- Black Lives Matter has more than forty official chapters worldwide.
- In 2016, #BlackLivesMatter became the third-biggest "social issues" hashtag in Twitter's history.

Simone Biles training on the floor exercise at the 2016 Rio Olympic Games. Simone would go on to win the gold on the floor event final, performing her signature move "The Biles," two flips in a straight body position with a half-twist.

A homemade Black Lives Matter protest sign made in January 2017 for the Women's March.

PATRISSE CULLORS

- Initially drawn to prison reform after witnessing incarcerated family members treated unjustly
- Founder of Dignity and Power Now

ALICIA GARZA

- Often uses the kitchen as a place to share ideas with friends and family for future activism
- A member of the inaugural class of Atlantic Fellows for Racial Equity, an organization dedicated to challenging anti-Black racism in the United States and South America

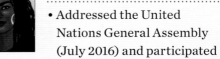

AYỌ TOMETI

- Addressed the United Nations General Assembly (July 2016) and participated in the UN's Global Forum on Migration and the Commission on the Status of Women (November 2017)
- Led and organized the first Congressional briefing on Black immigrants in Washington, DC (November 2017)

Ruby Bridges speaking at the 2015 Mayo Speaker Series held at Texas A&M University.

RUBY BRIDGES

- On November 14, 1960, became the first African American child (in modern times) to attend an all-white public elementary school in the American South
- Due to the chaos outside school, Ruby's first day of class was held in the principal's office.
- Federal marshals escorted Ruby down the hall for bathroom breaks.
- Dr. Robert Coles, a child psychiatrist, met with Ruby once a week during her first year at Frantz Elementary School to help her adjust.
- A statue of Ruby Bridges stands at Frantz Elementary School.

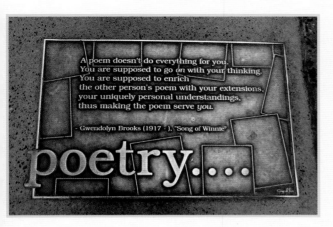

A quote from Gwendolyn Brooks featured on Library Way, a strip of sidewalk located on East 41st Street between Park Avenue and Fifth Avenue in New York City. Library Way was created in 1996 and features writing by a collection of prominent writers.

GWENDOLYN BROOKS

- Described her poems as "folksy narrative" and played with forms such as free verse, sonnets, epics, vignettes, and more
- Received support and encouragement from notable writers Langston Hughes, James Weldon Johnson, and Richard Wright
- Received the American Academy of Arts and Letters Award, the Robert Frost Medal, a National Endowment for the Arts Award, the Shelley Memorial Award, fellowships from the Academy of American Poets and the Guggenheim Foundation, and more than seventy honorary degrees from colleges across the United States
- Personal papers can be found at the Bancroft Library at UC Berkeley, as well as the University of Illinois Urbana-Champaign

ELIZABETH CATLETT

- Granddaughter of freed slaves and grew up hearing stories about the injustices of plantation life
- In addition to sculpture, made lithographs, screen prints, woodcuts, and linoleum cuts; appreciated that prints could be cheaply made and easily distributed
- Created likenesses of Angela Davis, Dr. Martin Luther King Jr., Malcolm X, Sojourner Truth, Harriet Tubman, and Phillis Wheatley, among others
- Continued making art through her mid-nineties

A photograph of Elizabeth Catlett's *Students Aspire* bronze relief installed in 1977 on the Howard University campus in Washington, DC.

Campaign buttons spreading the word about Shirley Chisholm's 1972 presidential run.

SHIRLEY CHISHOLM

- A founding member of the Congressional Black Caucus and the National Women's Political Caucus

- Campaign slogans: "Unbought and Unbossed," "Catalyst for Change," "To Represent All Americans," "Bring U.S. Together"
- Autobiography: *Unbought and Unbossed*. Memoir about Shirley's presidential campaign: *The Good Fight*.

Bessie Coleman, the first African American licensed pilot, shown here on the wheel of a Curtiss JN-4 "Jennie" (circa 1924).

BESSIE COLEMAN

- Skilled at mathematics as a child
- Refused to perform air shows unless the crowds were desegregated, an anomaly for the time
- Often flew Curtiss JN-4 planes
- Honored on the anniversary of her death by African American pilots, who fly over her grave and drop flowers
- US Postal Service issued a Bessie Coleman stamp in 1995 as part of their Black Heritage series

MISTY COPELAND

- Notable roles include the title role in *Firebird* (2012), Clara in *The Nutcracker*

(2014), Juliet in *Romeo & Juliet* (2015), and the first Black woman at American Ballet Theater to perform the lead role of Odette/Odile in *Swan Lake* (2014)
- Made her Broadway debut in 2014 as Ivy Smith in the musical *On the Town*
- Trains eight hours a day, six days a week during the American Ballet Theater season

Misty Copeland displaying her beautiful extension in a March 2014 performance of *Coppelia*, a comic ballet about a lifelike doll.

A passionate advocate and leader for civil rights, this poster captures Angela Davis speaking in 1965.

ANGELA DAVIS

- At the University of California at Santa Cruz, teaches in the Humanities, History of Consciousness, and Feminist Studies departments

- Has lectured in all fifty states, Africa, Europe, the Caribbean, and the former Soviet Union
- Author of nine books, including *Women, Race & Class,* and *Are Prisons Obsolete?*
- Subject of a number of documentary films, including *Free Angela and All Political Prisoners*

RUBY DEE

- Received an Emmy, a Grammy, and a Screen Actors Guild Award, as well as an Oscar nomination
- Author of two children's books, *Two Ways to Count to Ten* and *Tower to Heaven,* and several adult titles, including a memoir with her husband, *With Ossie and Ruby: In This Life Together*
- With Ossie, received the National Civil Rights Museum's Freedom Award for their protests of the police shooting of Amadou Diallo, an unarmed immigrant
- On August 29, 2014, Broadway dimmed theater lights to honor Ruby's passing.

Ava DuVernay (right) with actress Lupita Nyong'o (left) after winning a Peabody Award for her directorial work on the documentary *13th* on May 20, 2017.

AVA DuVERNAY

- First Black female director to have a film nominated for a Golden Globe or an Academy Award (*Selma*)
- Received second Oscar nomination in 2017 for *13th* in the Best Documentary Feature Film category
- Strives to employ a diverse cast and crew on all of her projects
- Actively works to create a movie set where actors, producers, crew members, and craft services are on equal footing
- Directed the 2017 music video "Family Feud" for Jay-Z, featuring Beyoncé
- Mattel created a Barbie doll in DuVernay's likeness.

ELLA FITZGERALD

- Nicknames: Lady Ella, the Queen of Jazz, First Lady of Song

Ella Fitzgerald in New York City circa November 1946.

- Was initially going to dance during her audition at the Apollo Theater. Ella was too afraid to move, so she sang instead.
- First international hit: "A-Tisket, A-Tasket," inspired by the nursery rhyme
- Won fourteen Grammy Awards, the National Medal of Arts, and the Presidential Medal of Freedom, among many other honors

ARETHA FRANKLIN

- Recorded her first gospel album (*Songs of Faith*) at age fourteen

- Duke Ellington, Ella Fitzgerald, Mahalia Jackson, and Clara Ward were among many famous household visitors.
- Invited Dr. Martin Luther King Jr. to the June 1963 Walk to Freedom march in Detroit as a result of her support of the civil rights movement
- The first woman inducted into the Rock and Roll Hall of Fame, in 1987
- Received the Presidential Medal of Freedom, eighteen Grammy Awards, the Grammy Lifetime Achievement Award, and a tribute from the American Music Awards
- Sang at Rosa Parks's funeral service on November 2, 2005

A poster for the Apollo Theater in Harlem, New York, advertising Aretha Franklin alongside fellow performers Brook Benton, the Flamingos, Sam Cook, and more.

ALTHEA GIBSON

- Won the New York City women's paddle tennis championship at age twelve
- First African American to win a Grand Slam championship
- Won the French Open in 1956
- Won six single Grand Slam titles, including the US Open and Wimbledon in 1957 and 1958
- First African American woman to appear on the cover of *Time* (August 26, 1957) and *Sports Illustrated* (September 2, 1957)
- In 1957, became the first Black woman to be voted Female Athlete of the Year by the Associated Press; earned the title again in 1958
- First African American to join the Ladies Professional Golf Association tour, in 1964
- Inducted into the International Women's Sports Hall of Fame and the International Tennis Hall of Fame

Professional tennis player Althea Gibson pictured with her tennis racket in 1956.

FANNIE LOU HAMER

- Although she only had six years of formal schooling, Fannie loved reading and reciting poetry
- Favorite song: "This Little Light of Mine"
- Cofounder of the Mississippi Freedom Democratic Party, established in 1964
- A post office and a public library in Mississippi have been named after Fannie.

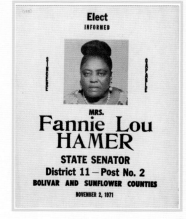

1971 election poster for Fannie Lou Hamer, candidate for Democratic state senator.

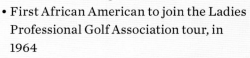

The Main Reading Room at the Library of Congress, one of the many facilities that Librarian of Congress Carla Hayden gets to consider her office.

CARLA HAYDEN

- President of the American Library Association from 2003 to 2004
- First Librarian of Congress to serve under a ten-year term; until 2015, position was a lifetime appointment
- Named a top leader in the world by *Forbes* in 2016

DOROTHY IRENE HEIGHT

- Credited as the first person to merge the fight for women's equality and equality for African Americans
- Active in international civil rights work in India and South Africa in addition to her participation in the US civil rights movement
- National president of the Delta Sigma Theta sorority from 1946 to 1957
- Founded the National Women's Political Caucus in 1971 with Gloria Steinem, Shirley Chisholm, and Betty Friedan, among others

- Winner of the Presidential Medal of Freedom and the Congressional Gold Medal

LENA HORNE

- Used her own money to perform for troops during World War II and refused to play shows where Black soldiers were not invited or were seated at the back of the audience
- Involved in civil rights activism for African Americans and Japanese Americans who faced discrimination during World War II
- Appeared as herself on popular television programs, including *Sanford & Son, The Muppet Show,* and *American Horror Story*
- Accepted an honorary degree from Howard University in 1980 after turning down similar offers. Lena said, "By the time Howard presented the doctorate to me, I knew I had graduated from the school of life, and I was ready to accept it."

A green velvet dress worn by Lena Horne during her portrayal of the character Selina Rogers in the 1943 film *Stormy Weather.*

ZORA NEALE HURSTON

- In 1917, lied about her age, saying she was sixteen instead of twenty-six in order to get free public schooling and finish her high school degree

A signed first edition of Zora Neale Hurston's magnum opus, first published in 1937.

- Traveled extensively through South America and the Caribbean for her anthropology fieldwork, including studying voodoo in Haiti on a Guggenheim Fellowship
- Grave unmarked for years until celebrated writer and fan Alice Walker purchased headstone that reads "Zora Neale Hurston: A Genius of the South."

on a fifty-city global tour to celebrate the company's fiftieth anniversary in 2008, and on two historic residencies in South Africa
- Credited with bringing financial stability to the Alvin Ailey American Dance Theater
- Autobiograpy titled *Dancing Spirit*

An embossed leather name tag for astronaut Mae Jemison.

JUDITH JAMISON

- Performed "Cry," choreographed by Alvin Ailey, for the first time from start to finish at the premiere, and received a standing ovation

Designed by Randy Barcelo, Judith Jamison wore this red costume during a ballet created by Alvin Ailey as part of a collaborative work with Duke Ellington.

- Learned over seventy ballets and performed in some of Ailey's most renowned works, including *Blues Suite* and *Revelations*
- Under her leadership, brought the Alvin Ailey American Dance Theater to its permanent home, the Joan Weill Center for Dance in Manhattan, the largest building in the United States devoted to dance
- Took the Alvin Ailey American Dance Theater

MAE C. JEMISON

- Logged 190 hours, 30 minutes, 23 seconds in space
- Favorite books as a kid were *A Wrinkle in Time* and *The Arm of the Starfish* by Madeleine L'Engle because they featured women heroines and scientists
- Proficient in Russian, Swahili, and Japanese
- Appeared on *Star Trek,* the first astronaut to do so, and has a Lego figurine in her likeness

KATHERINE JOHNSON

- Mentored by noted African American mathematician Dr. William W. Schieffelin Claytor, who made Johnson take every mathematics course in the college catalog and even created a class specifically for her

"Human computer" Katherine Johnson working at NASA circa 1966.

- In 1997, named Mathematician of the Year by the National Technical Association
- Celebrated her 100th birthday on August 26, 2018

Button commemorating Barbara Jordan's keynote address at the 1992 Democratic National Convention.

BARBARA JORDAN

- Worked on John F. Kennedy's 1960 presidential campaign
- Appointed by President Bill Clinton to head the Commission on Immigration Reform in 1994
- Honored with a statue in her likeness at the University of Texas at Austin
- Regarded as one of the greatest public speakers of the twentieth century

BEYONCÉ KNOWLES-CARTER

- Performed "At Last" at President Obama's 2009 inaugural ball and the national anthem at his 2013 inauguration
- Fan base called the BeyHive
- Has sold more than 100 million records worldwide

- Beyoncé and her younger sister, Solange, are the first sisters to both have number one albums

ANN LOWE

- Covered Paris's Fashion Week in 1947 on assignment from the *New York World-Telegram,* a renowned African American newspaper
- Lowe and her staff took eight weeks to make gowns for Bouvier-Kennedy bridal party; when ten gowns were ruined in a flood, they had five days to re-create them in time for the wedding
- At the peak of her career, Lowe's shop created more than a thousand dresses per year
- Good friends with Christian Dior

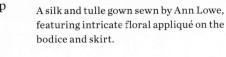
A silk and tulle gown sewn by Ann Lowe, featuring intricate floral appliqué on the bodice and skirt.

LORETTA LYNCH

- Considers Brooklyn, New York, her adopted home
- Directed the senior class play and was president of the literary club in high school

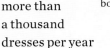

US Attorney General Loretta Lynch's official portrait, taken on June 29, 2015, by the United States Department of Justice.

- Professional achievements include working on the indictment of FIFA top officials and executives for money laundering and racketeering, announcing federal marriage benefits will extend to same-sex couples, assisting the DOJ's lawsuit against North Carolina's "bathroom bill," and leading Amazon's racial equity audit
- Was a member of the Harvard cheerleading team as an undergrad

IBTIHAJ MUHAMMAD

- Appeared on *Ellen* and *The Late Show with Stephen Colbert,* and taught First Lady Michelle Obama how to fence
- Ibtihaj Muhammad Day celebrated on September 10, 2016, in Maplewood, NJ
- Created nonprofit organization Athletes for Impact, connecting athletes with community initiatives for positive change

Ibtihaj Muhammad at the 2013 World Fencing Championships at Syma Hall in Budapest.

TONI MORRISON

- Wrote her debut novel, *The Bluest Eye,* at age thirty-nine
- When *Beloved* did not win the National Book Award, the *New York Times* published a letter of protest that was written and signed by forty-eight Black authors.
- As an editor at Random House, advanced the publishing careers of Angela Davis and Toni Cade Bambara
- An outspoken critic of police brutality and social injustice against Black men and women in America

An oil painting of First Lady Michelle Obama painted by Amy Sherald in 2018, on display at the National Portrait Gallery.

MICHELLE OBAMA

- As a child, loved cooking in her Easy-Bake Oven
- Favorite books growing up included *Pippi Longstocking* and *The Snowy Day* by Ezra Jack Keats
- Michelle and Barack's first date: seeing Spike Lee's *Do the Right Thing*
- First wedding dance song was "Unforgettable" by Nat King Cole
- Tied with Eleanor Roosevelt as the tallest First Ladies (5'11")
- Secret Service referred to Michelle with the code name Renaissance; Barack's was Renegade.

ROSA PARKS

- Autobiography: *Rosa Parks: My Story*
- A collection of Rosa's private correspondence, including letters to family members and a record of her work with activist organizations, is housed at the Library of Congress in Washington, DC.
- On the fiftieth anniversary of her arrest, several American cities, including New York and Washington, DC, left seats open on their public buses in her honor.

A bronze statue of Rosa Parks refusing to give up her seat to a white passenger. It is the first full-length statue of an African American to be displayed in the US Capitol.

LEONTYNE PRICE

- Nicknames: Our Empress, Our Queen
- Eleven southern cities refused to air Leontyne's televised performance of *Tosca* in 1955 because of racial prejudice.
- Performed at Carnegie Hall fifty times; her last performance there was in October 2001 to sing "America the Beautiful" as a tribute to those who lost their lives in the September 11 terrorist attacks

This oil painting depicting Leontyne Price was created in 1963 by artist Bradley Phillips and is now part of the National Portrait Gallery collection.

CONDOLEEZZA RICE

- Accompanied Yo-Yo Ma on piano at the 2002 National Medal of Arts Awards ceremony in Constitution Hall, and accompanied Aretha Franklin and the Philadelphia Orchestra at a 2010 benefit concert
- In 2012, became one of the first female members of the Augusta National Golf Club
- Author of numerous books, including her memoirs *Extraordinary, Ordinary People* and *No Higher Honor*
- A member of the 2013 College Football Playoff selection committee

The Benjamin Franklin State Dining Room is just one of many diplomatic reception rooms in the Harry S. Truman Federal Building. Secretary of State Condoleezza Rice worked out of this building and would often meet with foreign dignitaries as part of her duties.

A protest poster created by Faith Ringgold in 1971.

FAITH RINGGOLD

- Thurgood Marshall, Dinah Washington, Mary McLeod Bethune, and Duke Ellington were among the guests in her childhood home.
- In addition to quilts, created hooded masks, sculptures, fabric dolls, and performance art pieces
- Took Ringgold one month to make her quilt *Tar Beach,* now part of the collection at the Guggenheim Museum in New York City

DIANA ROSS

- Awards include the Presidential Medal of Freedom, Kennedy Center Honors, induction into the Rock & Roll Hall of Fame, and named Female Entertainer of the Century by *Billboard* magazine
- Has two stars on the Hollywood Walk of Fame: one for the Supremes and one for her solo work
- Film and Broadway play *Dreamgirls* loosely based on Motown and the legacy of the Supremes

Diana Ross's costume in the 1972 film *Lady Sings the Blues.* Diana portrayed legendary jazz singer Billie Holiday in the biopic.

WILMA RUDOLPH

- Nicknames: The Tornado, Skeeter (short for Mosquito)
- Overcame polio as a child
- Never lost a track meet in high school
- In college, once arrived to track practice thirty minutes late. As punishment, Wilma ran thirty laps, one for each minute she was late. The next day, Wilma was thirty minutes early for practice.

On October 4, 1960, Clarksville, Tennessee, celebrated Wilma Rudolph Day to celebrate her successes at the 1960 Summer Olympics. This souvenir program captures the event.

- First woman to win three gold medals at a single Olympic Games, in track and field
- Favorite event from the 1960 Olympic Games was the 4x100 meter relay because she got to share the podium with her Tennessee State University teammates; TSU sent forty women to the 1960 Olympics
- At TSU, the indoor track and a dormitory are named in Wilma's honor.

AUGUSTA FELLS SAVAGE

- Considered one of the most prominent artists of the Harlem Renaissance
- As committed to teaching art as she was to creating art
- Most notable sculptures were of W. E. B. Du Bois, Marcus Garvey, and William Pickens
- Many of her sculptures were made of plaster and destroyed because she did not have the funds to cast them in a more durable material.

NTOZAKE SHANGE

- Much of Ntozake's work is intended to be seen or heard onstage, often accompanied by dancing and modern or "free" jazz music.
- An accomplished violinist and dancer
- Used nontraditional capitalization and spelling in her work to challenge conventions of the time
- Coined the term "choreopoem" to describe the combination of poetry, movement, and music in her play *for colored girls*

Augusta Fells Savage with her sculpture *Realization* created circa 1938 as part of the Works Progress Administration's Federal Art Project.

A synthetic satin and crepe dress from Ntozake Shange's Broadway production of *for colored girls*.

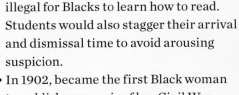

A promotional card advertising a 1954 performance by Eunice Waymon before she took on the stage name Nina Simone. Nina was twenty-one at this performance, and admission cost $1.30.

from seeing the true contents, as it was illegal for Blacks to learn how to read. Students would also stagger their arrival and dismissal time to avoid arousing suspicion.

- In 1902, became the first Black woman to publish a memoir of her Civil War experiences
- In addition to teaching, Taylor would also assist in maintaining guns for the officers, which included taking the gun apart, cleaning it, and putting it back together.

NINA SIMONE

- Known for improvising and interacting with the audience during her concerts
- President Barack Obama once listed Simone's rendition of "Sinnerman" as one of his ten favorite songs.
- Nicknames: the Civil Rights Diva, the High Priestess of Soul

SHERYL SWOOPES

- Her number 22 jersey was retired by Texas Tech, making Sheryl one of only three athletes to hold the honor.
- Appeared on a number of television shows, including *Martin, The Weakest Link,* and *Shirts & Skins*
- Collaborated with author Susan Kuklin to write *Hoops with Swoopes,* a basketball book for children

SUSIE KING TAYLOR

- As a child, would wrap her school books in paper to prevent police or whites

SOJOURNER TRUTH

- Best known for her improvised speech "Ain't I a Woman?" delivered at the 1851 Ohio Women's Rights Convention; later proven unlikely that Sojourner spoke the titular line at all, but the powerful sentiment remains
- Helped to recruit African American men to join the Union Army during the Civil War
- In 1865, attempted to desegregate streetcars in Washington, DC
- Believed the suffrage of women and African Americans should occur simultaneously

Photograph of Sojourner Truth, taken in 1863. On her lap she has a daguerreotype of her grandson James Caldwell, a member of the 54th Massachusetts Infantry Regiment.

A white silk and lace shawl owned by Harriet Tubman around the late 1890s.

family members and experimented with different ingredients until she perfected the formula

- A beautician, entrepreneur, and activist for African American rights; covered tuition costs for six African American students to attend the Tuskegee Institute; donated to the NAACP; traveled to Washington, DC, to advocate for federal anti-lynching legislation
- By 1916, Walker and her company were worth over $1 million dollars and employed 40,000 African American women across the US, Central America, and the Caribbean.

A convention badge for entrepreneur Madam C. J. Walker made from brass and created in the 1920s.

HARRIET TUBMAN

- Never lost a "passenger" while leading groups on the Underground Railroad; one of her riskiest trips was rescuing her aging parents
- By 1856, slave owners posted a reward of $40,000 for her capture.
- Harriet's intimate knowledge of the landscape, mastery of disguises, and other tricks that helped her thwart slave owners also made her a valuable spy for the Union Army during the Civil War.
- Regarded as the first Black woman to serve in the US military

IDA B. WELLS

- Nickname: The Princess of the Press
- Considered a pioneer of modern journalism because of her reporting skills
- Was a mentor to author W. E. B. Du Bois and was friends with abolitionist leader Frederick Douglass
- Never finished her autobiography, which was published posthumously as *Crusade for Justice: The Autobiography of Ida B. Wells*

MADAM C. J. WALKER

- Pioneered her hair pomade after experiencing her own hair loss; consulted with

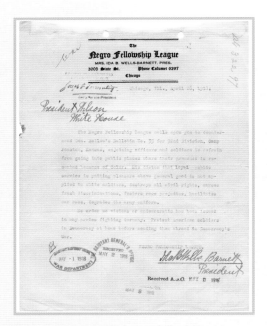

During her tenure as president of the Negro Fellowship League, Ida B. Wells sent this letter to President Woodrow Wilson, calling for him to retract an order that urged officers and soldiers in Camp Funston, Kansas, to avoid public locations as they were resented because of their skin color.

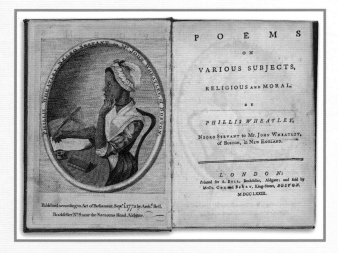

A copy of Phillis Wheatley's *Poems on Various Subjects, Religious and Moral*, first printed in London in 1773.

PHILLIS WHEATLEY

- Met with Benjamin Franklin during a trip to London to promote work
- Wrote an estimated 145 poems during her lifetime
- More widely acclaimed in Europe than the US because of racial prejudice

SERENA WILLIAMS

- Won the 2017 Australian Open while pregnant with daughter Alexis Olympia Ohanian Jr.
- Inspired the term Serena Slam, used to describe a player who consecutively wins the Australian Open, French Open, Wimbledon, and US Open but not in the same year/season
- Speaks French fluently

Sisters and doubles partners Venus and Serena Williams at the first round of the 2013 US Open.

VENUS AND SERENA WILLIAMS

- Opened the Yetunde Price Resource Center in 2016, named in honor of their sister, and provides resources to Compton, California, community members impacted by gun violence
- In 2009, became minority owners of the Miami Dolphins, the first Black women to have an ownership stake in an NFL franchise

- Venus prefers grass tennis courts; Serena likes clay surfaces.
- Have more Olympic gold medals than any other tennis players in history, male or female, with four each

The Oprah Winfrey exhibit at the Smithsonian National Museum of African American History and Culture. The archway even incorporates the signature "O" design.

OPRAH WINFREY

- Given name is Orpah, from the Bible, but because of misspellings and mispronunciations was called Oprah from an early age
- Was fired from a job as an evening news reporter, told she was "unfit for television news"; made her daytime television program, which was meant to be a demotion, wildly successful
- Credits notable Chicago-based movie critic Roger Ebert with convincing her to take *The Oprah Winfrey Show* into syndication
- One of the first Black women to appear on the cover of *Vogue*
- The only Black billionaire in North America

Image Credits

Randi Charno Levine and Jeffrey E. Levine; Fred M. Levin and Nancy Livingston; The Shenson Foundation; Monique Meloche Gallery, Chicago; Arthur Lewis and Hau Nguyen; Sara and John Schram; Alyssa Taubman and Robert Rothman. 115 left. 115 right: art © Bradley Phillips, gift of Ms. Sayre Sheldon.

SMITHSONIAN INSTITUTION ARCHIVES

104 left: photo © by Robert S. Scurlock, Scurlock Studio Records, ca. 1905–1994, Archives Center, National Museum of American History. 106 left. 108 bottom right: art design © by Richard McCrary for the New York Committee to Free Angela Davis, New York, 1971. 120 top left: National Archives at College Park.

SMITHSONIAN NATIONAL AIR AND SPACE MUSEUM

112 right: transfer from NASA Data Service.

SMITHSONIAN NATIONAL MUSEUM OF AFRICAN AMERICAN HISTORY AND CULTURE

111 right. 112 top left. 112 bottom left. 116 right. 118 left. 118 right. 120 bottom left. 121. 123 bottom right.

SMITHSONIAN NATIONAL MUSEUM OF AFRICAN AMERICAN HISTORY AND CULTURE, GIFTS

107 bottom right (both), 123 top right, 124 middle right: Dawn Simon Spears and Alvin Spears, Sr. 110 left: Lydia Samuel Bennett. 113 left: Anonymous gift. 113 right, 117 right, 124 top left, 124 bottom left: the Black Fashion Museum founded by Lois K. Alexander-Lane. 117 top left: the Rudolph Family in memory of Wilma Rudolph. 119 left: Charles L. Blockson. 119 right:

Dr. Patricia Heaston. 123 left: with pride from Ellen Brooks. 123 middle right: the Estate of Ella Fitzgerald. 124 top right: Charles L. Blockson. 124 bottom right: Oprah Winfrey.

WIKIPEDIA COMMONS

104 right: Kyle Tsui. 105 bottom left: Fernando Frazão/Agência Brasil. 105 right: Black Lives Matter organization. 106 right: Texas A&M University—Commerce Marketing Communications Photography. 107 left: Lesekreis. 107 top right: Takomabibelot. 108 left. 108 top right: Naim Chidiac, Abu Dhabi Festival. 109 left: Stephanie Moreno/Grady College of Journalism and Mass Communications for Peabody Awards/University of Georgia. 110 bottom right: Mississippi Department of Archives and History. 111 left: Carol M. Highsmith 2011. 114 left: United States Department of Justice. 114 top right: © Marie-Lan Nguyen. 117 bottom left: Andrew Herman. 120 right: Edwin Martinez. 127: Prabal.tiwari1993.

Visit the achievements and memorabilia of the women in this book at the Smithsonian Museums. You can also find them online at:

- Smithsonian National Air and Space Museum: airandspace.si.edu
- Smithsonian National Museum of American History: americanhistory.si.edu
- Smithsonian Anacostia Community Museum: anacostia.si.edu
- Smithsonian National Portrait Gallery: npg.si.edu

At the National Museum of African American History and Culture

- The black velvet skirt and the decorative trim from the jacket **Marian Anderson** wore at the April 9, 1939, Lincoln Memorial performance
- A newspaper clipping from the *New York Times* reviewing *I Know Why the Caged Bird Sings* by **Maya Angelou**
- A photograph of **Mary McLeod Bethune**'s statue in Lincoln Park, Washington, DC, taken by Milton Williams in 1974
- A **Black Lives Matter** T-shirt from 2015, also featuring other slogans associated with the movement, including "Hands Up, Don't Shoot"
- A paperback edition of **Gwendolyn Brooks**'s *Riot*, a poem told in three parts; her novel *Black Steel: Joe Frazier and Muhammad Ali;* and a first-edition hardcover of *Annie Allen*

A Shirley Chisholm presidential campaign poster.

- ★ **Shirley Chisholm**'s 1972 presidential campaign poster that reads "Bring U.S. Together" and 1972 presidential campaign buttons that include the slogans "Unbought and Unbossed," "Let's Get to the Chisholm of the Problem," and "Catalyst for Change," as well as her autobiography *Unbought and Unbossed*
- Prints of famous history makers like **Sojourner Truth, Harriet Tubman,** and **Phillis Wheatley** created by artist **Elizabeth Catlett**
- ★ A button featuring airwoman **Bessie Coleman** from the mid to late twentieth century

- **Angela Davis**'s FBI Wanted poster issued in 1970, and a pin commemorating "Angela Is Free"
- The 1961 lobby card for *A Raisin in the Sun* and *St. Louis Blues,* both featuring actress **Ruby Dee**
- **Ava DuVernay**'s short film titled *August 28: A Day in the Life of a People,* which tracks significant moments in African American history that occurred on this date over decades
- ★ **Ella Fitzgerald**'s marigold cocktail dress designed by Don Loper
- A Stevie Wonder songbook, *Stevie Wonder Thought Shares,* featuring the work of **Aretha Franklin,** among others
- ★ **Althea Gibson**'s 1957 Wightman Cup medal and blazer, 1995 American Tennis Association membership card, and tennis racket cover
- A photograph of **Fannie Lou Hamer** speaking at Freedom Day in Hattiesburg, Mississippi, taken by Louis H. Draper in 1964
- **Dorothy Irene Height** on the cover of *Tuesday Magazine* in March 1970

The photo in this Bessie Coleman pin is the same one used on her pilot's license issued by the Fédération Aéronautique Internationale.

A dress worn by Ella Fitzgerald in the 1950s.

An off-white blazer gifted to Althea Gibson in 1957, courtesy of the United States Tennis Association.

- **Lena Horne**'s dresser set, including her hand mirror, hairbrush, and nail file, among other items; a poster advertising her performance at the Olympia Music Hall in 1954; and the green velvet dress she wore in the film *Stormy Weather*
- A signed first-edition hardcover of *Their Eyes Were Watching God* by **Zora Neale Hurston**

Ann Lowe designed this pink satin and organza dress in 1959.

- A commemorative pin from **Mae Jemison**'s space shuttle mission STS-47
- A photograph of NASA pioneer **Katherine Johnson** taken by Annie Leibovitz in 2016
- A pin advertising 1992 Democratic National Convention speaker **Barbara Jordan**
- ★ Several dresses made in the 1960s by seamstress and stylist **Ann Lowe** featuring her intricate silk flower work
- Photographs of **Toni Morrison** with her sons, Harold Ford Morrison and Slade Morrison, taken by Jack Mitchell in 1978
- A photograph of former President Barack Obama and First Lady **Michelle Obama** taken by Mariana Cook in 1996
- ★ **Rosa Parks**, photographed in 1991 by Roderick J. Lyons, and a dress she sewed between 1955 and 1956
- **Faith Ringgold**'s evocative poster calling for **Angela Davis**'s freedom (1971)
- A copy of *Diana Ross and The Supremes & The Temptations on Broadway: Original TV Soundtrack,* released in 1969

Rosa Parks sewed this belted wrap dress between 1955 and 1956. The dress is made from a plain weave viscose fabric with a yellow and brown flower and leaf pattern.

- A souvenir program celebrating **Wilma Rudolph** Day on October 4, 1960, in Clarksville, Tennessee
- The playbill from **Ntozake Shange**'s November 1977 production of *for colored girls* and the costumes for the Lady in Purple, the Lady in Orange, and the Lady in Red
- **Nina Simone**'s 1964 record *Mississippi *@!!?*@!* and *Sea Lion Woman,* a card promoting her piano recital in 1954 when she was still using her birth name Eunice Waymon, and photographs of her singing at Symphony Hall in Boston in 1969
- An 1863 portrait of **Sojourner Truth,** as well as her carte de visite and cabinet card
- ★ **Harriet Tubman**'s gospel hymn book, handkerchief, silk lace and linen shawl, and a brick from her home
- ★ A tin of **Madam C. J. Walker**'s Wonderful Hair Grower, and her convention badge from the 1920s
- A statue of **Venus and Serena Williams** and photographs of the girls playing tennis in 1991
- ★ **Oprah Winfrey**'s gold microphone used during season 24 of *The Oprah Winfrey Show,* and three red giant bows from her famous car giveaway

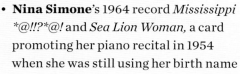

Harriet Tubman's hymnal.

Madam C. J. Walker's Wonderful Hair Grower was sold in the 1910s and 1920s.

One of Oprah's microphones.

At the National Portrait Gallery

- An oil painting of **Marian Anderson** in front of the Lincoln Memorial before her famous concert, by Betsy Graves Reyneau in 1955
- A headshot of **Maya Angelou,** taken by Brigitte Lacombe in 1987
- An oil painting of **Mary McLeod Bethune,** by Betsy Graves Reyneau in 1943
- A bronze bust of **Gwendolyn Brooks,** by Sara S. Miller in 1994
- A photograph of **Elizabeth Catlett** with one of her sculpted pieces, taken by Mariana Yampolsky in 1949
- A photograph of **Shirley Chisholm,** taken by Richard Avedon on July 12, 1976
- A screen print on foil of **Angela Davis,** by **Elizabeth Catlett** in 1972
- A photograph of **Ruby Dee** with her husband, Ossie Davis, taken by Anthony Barboza in 1977
- A photograph of **Ella Fitzgerald** at the mic with Ray Brown, Dizzy Gillespie, and Milt Jackson, taken by William Paul Gottlieb in 1947
- A poster advertising **Aretha Franklin,** by Milton Glaser in 1968
- A watercolor and graphite painting of **Althea Gibson** with a tennis ball, by Boris Chaliapin in 1957
- A photograph of **Fannie Lou Hamer** singing, taken by Charmain Reading in 1966
- An oil painting of **Lena Horne** in an evening gown, by Edward Biberman in 1947
- A photograph of **Judith Jamison** performing the dance "Cry," taken by Max Walden in 1976
- A photograph of **Barbara Jordan,** taken by Richard Avedon on July 14, 1976
- An advertisement for **Beyoncé Knowles-Carter**'s *Dangerous in Love* CD, by Markus Klinko and Indrani Pal-Chaudhuri in 2003
- A photograph of **Toni Morrison,** taken by Helen Marcus in 1978
- An oil painting of former First Lady **Michelle Obama,** by Amy Sherald in 2018
- A limewood painted sculpture of **Rosa Parks** with police officers, by Marshall D. Rumbaugh in 1983
- A screen print with rhinestones of **Condoleezza Rice** titled *When Ends Meet,* made by Mickalene Thomas in 2007 and 2008
- A hand-painted quilt made by **Faith Ringgold** in 1998, documenting moments in her Harlem childhood, based on her autobiographical book *Seven Passages to a Flight*
- A photograph of **Diana Ross** with Florence Ballard and Mary Wilson, taken by Bruce Davidson in 1965
- A photograph of **Wilma Rudolph** racing, taken by George Silk in 1960
- A photograph of **Ntozake Shange,** taken by Anthony Barboza in 1977
- A photograph of **Sojourner Truth,** taken by Randall Studio circa 1870
- A photograph of **Harriet Tubman,** taken by H. Seymour Squyer circa 1885
- A photograph of **Ida B. Wells,** taken by Sallie E. Garrity circa 1893
- A paper engraving of **Phillis Wheatley,** created in 1773 by an unknown illustrator
- A photograph of **Venus and Serena Williams,** taken by Annie Leibovitz in 1998
- A photograph of **Oprah Winfrey,** taken by Brigitte Lacombe in 2009

About the National Museum of African American History and Culture

The National Museum of African American History and Culture opened in September 2016 as the nineteenth museum of the Smithsonian Institution, the largest museum complex and research organization in the world. To date, the museum has welcomed more than five million visitors and is proud to be the nation's largest and most comprehensive cultural destination devoted exclusively to exploring, documenting, and showcasing the African American story and its impact on American and world history.

The National Museum of African American History and Culture was designed by the Freelon Adjaye Bond/SmithGroup and headed by lead designer David Adjaye and lead architect Philip Freelon. The museum's distinctive three tiers, or corona, were inspired by crowns used in Yoruban art from West Africa.

You can visit the National Museum of African American History and Culture in Washington, DC, and online at nmaahc.si.edu.

Index